Leading Groups and Teams

Managerial Communication Series

By: **Bonnie T. Yarbrough**
University of North Carolina, Greensboro

Series Editor: **James S. O'Rourke, IV**
University of Notre Dame

THOMSON
SOUTH-WESTERN

Australia · Canada · Mexico · Singapore · Spain · United Kingdom · United States

To my family:
Pam, Colleen, Molly, and Kathleen.
And to my colleagues:
Carolyn, Sandra, Cynthia, and Renee.
Thanks.
JSO'R, IV

To Stephen and Anna, and to my mother, Hanna.
BTY

Leading Groups and Teams, Managerial Communication Series
James S. O'Rourke, IV, series editor; Bonnie T. Yarbrough, author

VP/Editor-in-Chief: Jack Calhoun	**Production Editor:** Robert Dreas	**Design Project Manager:** Michelle Kunkler
VP/Team Director: Melissa Acuña	**Manufacturing Coordinator:** Diane Lohman	**Cover and Internal Designer:** Robb and Associates
Developmental Editor: Taney Wilkins	**Compositor:** Lachina Publishing Services	**Cover Illustration:** © Artville/Richard Cook
Marketing Manager: Larry Qualls	**Printer:** Victor Graphics, Inc., Baltimore, Maryland	

COPYRIGHT © 2003
by South-Western, a division of Thomson Learning. Thomson
Learning™ is a trademark used herein under license.

ISBN: 0-324-15254-X
Printed in Canada
1 2 3 4 5 04 03 02 01

For more information contact South-Western, 5191 Natorp
Boulevard, Mason, Ohio 45040. Or you can visit our Internet site
at: http://www.swcollege.com

For permission to use material from this text or product, contact us by
Tel (800) 730-2214
Fax (800) 730-2215
http://www.thomsonrights.com

Library of Congress Cataloging-in-Publication Data

Yarbrough, Bonnie T., (Bonnie Thames)
  Leading groups and teams / by Bonnie T. Yarbrough.
    p. cm. -- (Managerial communication series ; 1)
  Includes bibliographical references and index.
  ISBN 0-324-15254-X
  1. Teams in the workplace--Management. 2. Communication in
management. I. Title. II. Series.
  HD66 .L434 2001
  658.4'036--dc21

                    2001057783

AUTHOR BIOGRAPHIES

James Scofield O'Rourke, IV, is director of the Eugene D. Fanning Center for Business Communication at the University of Notre Dame, where he teaches writing and speaking. In a thirty-five year career, he has earned an international reputation in business and corporate communication. *Business Week* magazine again named him one of the "outstanding faculty" in Notre Dame's Mendoza College of Business. Professor O'Rourke has held faculty appointments in such schools as the United States Air Force Academy, the Defense Information School, the United States Air War College, and the Communication Institute of Ireland. He is a regular consultant to Fortune 500 and mid-size businesses, and is widely published in both professional journals and the popular press.

Bonnie Thames Yarbrough currently teaches management communications and advanced topics in communications for the MBA program in the Joseph M. Bryan School of Business and Economics, as well as academic and professional communication for the graduate school at the University of North Carolina at Greensboro. She also teaches other courses, including business communications and diversity in the workplace, in the Department of Business Administration. She has extensive experience in program development, curriculum design, training workshops, negotiation, grant writing, leadership, and consulting throughout her professional and academic career. As the communication specialist for the Program for Management Development at UNC Greensboro, she trains managers and executives in communication, negotiation, and diversity skills, and often works with business and civic organizations.

TABLE OF CONTENTS

FOREWORD

In recent years, for a variety of reasons, communication has grown increasingly complex. The issues that seemed so straightforward, so simple not long ago, are now somehow different, more complicated. Has the process changed? Have the elements of communication, or the barriers to success, been altered? What's different now? Why has this all gotten more difficult?

Several issues are at work here, not the least of which is pacing. Information, images, events, and human activity all move at a much faster pace than they did just a decade ago. The most popular new business magazine is *Fast Company*. Readers are reminded that it's not just a matter of tempo, but a new way of living we're experiencing.

Technology has changed things as well. We're now able to communicate with almost anyone, almost anywhere, 24/7, with very little effort and very little professional assistance. It's all possible because of cellular telephone technology, digital imaging, the Internet, fiber optics, global positioning satellites, teleconferencing codecs, high-speed data processing, online data storage, and . . . well, the list goes on and on. What's new this morning will be old hat by lunch.

Culture has intervened in our lives in some important ways. Very few parts of the world are inaccessible any more. Other people's beliefs, practices, perspectives, and possessions are as familiar to us as our own. And for many of us, we're only now coming to grips with the idea that our own beliefs aren't shared by everyone and that culture is hardly value-neutral.

The nature of the world in which we live—one that's wired, connected, mobile, fast-paced, iconically visual, and far less driven by logic—has changed in some not-so-subtle ways in recent days. The organizations that employ us and the businesses that depend on our skills now recognize that communication is at the center of what it means to be successful—and at the heart of what it means to be human.

To operate profitably means that business must now conduct itself in responsible ways, and be keenly attuned to the needs and interests of its stakeholders. And, more than ever, the communication skills and capabilities we bring to the workplace are essential to our success, both at the individual and at the societal level.

So, what does that mean to you as a prospective manager or executive in training? For one thing, it means that communication will involve more than simple writing, speaking, and listening skills. It will involve new contexts, new applications, and new technologies. Much of what will affect the balance of your life has yet to be invented. But when it is, you'll have to learn to live with it and make it work on your behalf.

The book you've just opened is the first of a series of six that will help you to do all of those things and more. It's direct, simple, and compact. The aim of my colleague, Professor Bonnie Yarbrough, is not to provide you with a broad-based education in either business or communication, but rather to pinpoint the issues and ideas most closely associated with successful communication in *Leading Groups and Teams*.

In the volumes that follow, Professor Carolyn Boulger will explore *e-Technology and the Fourth Economy*. With the help of renowned Swedish communication consultant Hans Johnsson, she will look at the emergence of a fundamental revolution in how people work, live, and earn a living. And she will examine how the new technologies have influenced and transformed all of that and more.

Professor Sandra Collins, a social psychologist by training, will explore *Communication in a Virtual Organization*. The conceptual framework she brings to the discussion will help you to understand how time and distance compression have altered work habits and collaboration. With the help of corporate communication executive and consultant Sixtus J. Oeschle, she will show you exciting, current examples of global companies and local groups that illustrate the ways in which our work and lives have permanently changed.

For the iconically challenged (I am one who thinks in words and phrases, not pictures), Professor Cynthia Maciejczyk, with the assistance of a number of artists and graphic technologists, will examine *Graphics and Visual Communication for Managers*. If you've ever wondered how to transform words and numbers into pictures, she can help. And for all of us who've ever tried to explain complex issues without success, either aloud or on paper, the message is simple: If you can't say it in a clear, compelling way, perhaps you can show them.

Professor Collins will also examine *Managing Conflict and Workplace Relationships* in a volume that may have more of a lasting impact on how (and with whom) we can work than any of the other titles. Her approach involves far more than dispute resolution or figuring out how limited resources can be distributed equitably among people who think they all deserve more. She shows us how to manage our own emotions, as well as those of others. Creative conflict, along with harmony and synchronicity in the workplace, are issues too many of us have avoided because we simply didn't understand them or didn't know what to say.

Finally, Professor Yarbrough will examine *International and Intercultural Communication*, looking both broadly and specifically at issues and opportunities that will seem increasingly important as the business world shrinks and grows more interdependent. As time zones blur and fewer restrictions are imposed on the global movement of capital, raw materials, finished goods, and human labor, people will cling fiercely to the ways in which they were enculturated as youngsters. Culture will become a defining characteristic, not only of peoples and nations, but of organizations and industries.

This is an interesting, exciting, and highly practical series of books. They're small, of course, intended not as comprehensive texts, but as supplemental readings, or as stand-alone volumes for modular courses or seminars. They're engaging because they've been written by people who are smart, passionate about what they do, and more than happy to share what they know. And I've been happy to edit the series, first, because these women are all friends and colleagues whom I know and have come to trust. Secondly, I've enjoyed the task because this is really interesting stuff. Read on. There is a lot to learn here, new horizons to explore, and new ways to think about human communication.

James S. O'Rourke, IV
The Eugene D. Fanning Center
Mendoza College of Business
University of Notre Dame
Notre Dame, Indiana

Managerial Communication Series

Editor: James S. O'Rourke, IV

*The **Managerial Communication Series** is a series of modules designed to teach students how to communicate and manage in today's competitive environment. Purchase only this module as a supplemental product for your Business Communication, Management, or other Business course, or purchase all six modules, packaged together at a discounted price for full coverage of Managerial Communication.*

ISBN: 0-324-15254-X

This text reviews the latest research on small group and team interaction, and offers practical advice on project management, intra-team conflict, and improving results. It contains group and team worksheets, progress reports, and sample reporting instruments, as well as classroom discussion questions and case studies.

ISBN: 0-324-15255-8

This text offers a radical new view of technology's impact on what the author calls "The Fourth Economy," an economic model based entirely on minds in interaction. Technology's role in helping participants in the radically transformed landscape of the twenty-first century is not limited to the transmission and storage of text and data, but extends to the very ways in which people think about and create value.

ISBN: 0-324-15256-6

This text explores the risks and opportunities open to those who work in new alliances, partnerships, and non-traditional business models. A look at both theory and practical application offers students and managers the chance to observe successful organizations in action. Foreword by Sixtus J. Oeschle of Shell Oil and Internet Pipeline.

ISBN: **0-324-16178-6**

This text offers some practical and useful advice on how to work with graphics and visuals in reports, briefings, and proposals. It also offers direct instruction on how to integrate graphic aids into spoken presentations and public speeches. If you can't say it or write it clearly, you may be able to show it. Dozens of illustrations, drawings, and graphs are included.

ISBN: **0-324-15257-4**

Learn what social scientists and business executives now know about conflict, personality style, organizational structure, and human interaction. Examine the most successful strategies for keeping your edge and keeping your friends. Practical forms, instruments, and applications are included.

ISBN: **0-324-15258-2**

This text examines the basis for culture, reviewing the work of social scientists, cultural anthropologists, and global managers on this emerging topic. Definitions of culture, issues of cultural change and how cultures adapt are included, along with practical examples, case studies, and illustrations of how cultural issues are managed both domestically and internationally. Factors ranging from power distance to social gender roles are examined in detail.

INTRODUCTION

Most of us have been members of some kind of team. Our team experiences have shaped our attitudes toward them, just as the frenzy of activity on this subject has shaped our management techniques over the last decade. Responses to using teams vary from sometimes glib dismissals to reverent confirmations of complex practices that have shaped the way products are developed, delivered, tested, redesigned, and improved. Lately, the responses have been so varied that we may wonder: What could possibly be left unexamined on the idea of using teams? This book offers some answers to that question for those still struggling with the single most difficult aspect of leading teams and groups: managing communication among members.

New information about ways to form, implement, and evaluate teams in the workplace has greatly refined our understanding of them. Studies too numerous to list here have defined, qualified, and classified groups, just as they have magnified distinctions in team performance and effectiveness among industries, functional areas, operational processes, and workplace behaviors. Literally hundreds of articles, books, and reports on teams have greatly increased our understanding of this most basic of human configurations.[1] Those reports, of course, are as varied in their approach and findings as the authors themselves. Perhaps the best reason for our continued fascination, whether as practitioners or researchers, is that this work is about *us*.

Research on teams and team practices in sometimes dissimilar disciplines and cultures has contributed greatly to the ongoing conversation. Whether in business settings, academic circles, communities of practice,[2] or self-help seminars, the word *team* calls to mind strong but very different responses. This text examines what we know about teams and suggests new ways of improving the team process. For those new to the team process, this may introduce a rich field of study. For those more experienced, it may remind you of things you weren't sure you knew.

The word **team** carries resonance, then, because of its nuances. For our purposes, a useful framework should not be contingent on any one viewpoint but should be flexible enough to apply to a range of groups. Whether defined as real or not, teams, as well as learning groups, communities, committees, organizations, and task forces, need people who understand basic principles of effective group communication and who understand that *individual* skills can enhance or inhibit team communication. Some of the examples we'll see in this book will illustrate communication challenges effective teams face, whether or not they are real or formal in any traditional sense. While panels, some committees, and focus groups, for example, often work collaboratively, they do not constitute real teams but are rather collections of individuals. What distinguishes the treatment here is our focus on teams within the context of communication, specifically, management communication.

Business schools have long recognized the importance of using the team approach in undergraduate and graduate business programs, but many still use early models based on team formation or team building.[3] Yet many schools that practice team-based assignments simply create pseudo-teams with artificial reasons for working together. When students are grouped together in teams, they have at least a clear, short-term goal: to do as well as they can on the assignment.

Put more clearly, most student teams want an "A." If those team members bond together in their class work with *only* this goal in mind (admirable though it is), they will employ an individual value system for a group task. In other words, they apply the same approach for each group assignment regardless of audience, mission, team skills, culture, or required tasks.

If a school—no matter what the level of instruction—fails to use a systematic set of guidelines for team projects, students as well as faculty will be disappointed by the results. For example, faculty who allow teams to self-select members yield responsibility for managing the team process: creating groups whose members can learn from one another, providing a shared mission, and offering strategies for teams to do their work. Understanding the challenges of implementing an effective group project often precludes friends working with friends, or spouses, or partners repeatedly in different settings. Working with the same group for no other reason than friendship also defeats the goal of developing flexible management skills and communication competencies. Such situations almost always produce another undesirable but preventable problem: Some people are never chosen. Faculties sometimes assign the unwelcome people to groups, which starts these receiving teams off on shaky ground. Any problem or conflict that may emerge later arises naturally from these additions.

Too often, success is measured by looking only at the end product (usually a report or a presentation), regardless of how many members were involved in producing it, or at reported information rather than the processes involved in implementing strategies. In such cases, teams learn very little about the team process and how to improve it other than understanding that they have to survive it and get the project done. After all, a simulation, regardless of how realistic the components may be, is still understood and experienced as a simulation.

The team communication (TeamComm) framework presented in this book encourages a broader understanding of the challenges inherent in work groups. Our aim is to develop more complex communication tools, clarify the scope of management competencies, and establish the expectation that managing teams will involve a lifelong, extended learning curve.

The debate about whether teams in university classes qualify as formal teams at all shouldn't prevent educators from using and developing them as valuable learning opportunities. As long as instructors clarify the goals, ensure that procedures are open and accessible, and explain the framework, TeamComm strategies can provide another useful option for implementing teams at this level.[4] If using teams makes good sense within the course context, the five-level framework still applies: Self, team, institution, culture, and delivery technology (media) are key components when designing, adapting, or reframing team assignments.

If students and managers alike work to apply team communication strategies with the same rigor that they apply to using teams, performance will improve for individuals as well as the team. After all, we know that the top three traits a manager needs are to listen effectively and counsel, to work well with others one on one, and to work cooperatively in small groups. Seen another way, a manager cannot hope to be effective without thoroughly understanding teamwork. For students, using effective team communication skills may provide the relevance needed not only for an engaging team experience but also for a competitive edge.

This brief book, then, presents a framework for leading teams that applies broadly to various learning organizations, companies, training programs, upper-level business communication classes, and graduate business programs that use management communication in complex ways. While mandating no single interpretation for these organizations, the TeamComm framework is flexible enough for managers and leaders to use in very different settings. Whether visual or virtual, teams are composed of humans who communicate—or fail to do so—through their values, assumptions, beliefs, procedures, and technologies.

This book contains many factual examples, anecdotes, and vignettes drawn from companies representing different industries, business sectors, and continents. These illustrate the universal need for good communication strategies as the key to successful teams.

- Chapter 1, Communication in Groups and Teams, examines work groups and teams as the most widely applied configurations in the workplace today. These groups have specific, accompanying communication needs arising from the team approach. The TeamComm framework introduced here describes a systems model for classifying communication challenges as they exist on five levels: self, team, institution, culture, and media. Along with the model, a number of different assessment tools provide a useful and efficient means of gathering information to form teams.

- Chapter 2, TeamComm Performance Strategies, extends the TeamComm framework to include a set of procedural strategies for establishing and managing communication protocol by using six functional opportunities the team process offers: connecting, defining, communicating, conflicting, energizing, and evaluating. Another set of team assessment tools provides a handy way of tracking team development and progress.

- Chapter 3, Strategies for Managing Team Conflict, addresses the essential issue of conflict by looking at specific ways to classify team conflict, to analyze individual conflict styles, and to identify strategies for encouraging healthy conflict practices. By examining seven areas where teams commonly fail, this chapter also provides guidelines for team communication success.

- We also offer small case studies for discussion and analysis from two companies facing very different and challenging team situations. Appendix A provides additional resources for conflict assessment and analysis, and Appendix B is a select bibliography.

Few of us work in pure fields, isolated from all others. Similarly, few true communication problems involve simple, one-way solutions. Effective group communication strategies are perhaps most useful if given a wide latitude within a shared system of understanding. Regardless of field, industry, functional area, or discipline, effective communication techniques require us to recognize and respect our interconnectedness in daily work in much the same way that good teams recognize and respect the interdependence of team members.

On the one hand, if we connect the dots between our shared perspectives, processes, and practices, we can appreciate the potential a team experience presents for strategic activities and applications. On the other hand, if we can construct meaningful and accessible images from those connections, we can grasp the power. Some of the ways to do that are in this book. But team*work* is still, after all, *work*. The rest is up to you.

ENDNOTES

1. For a partial list, see Select Bibliography at the end of the book. For a more thorough review of the research literature on teams from 1990–1996, see Susan Cohen and Diane E. Bailey, "What Makes Teams Work: Group Effectiveness Research from the Shop Floor to the Executive Suite," *Journal of Management* 23, no. 3 (1997): 239–290.

2. Etienne C. Wenger and William M. Snyder, "Communities of Practice: The Organizational Frontier," *Harvard Business Review,* January–February 2000, 139–145. Anne Donnellon treats the significance of talk in depth in *Team Talk: The Power of Language in Team Dynamics* (Boston: Harvard Business School Press, 2000).

3. See, for example, Bruce Tuckman's Orming Model in "Development Sequence in Small Groups," *Psychological Bulletin* 63, no. 6 (1965).

4. Larry K. Michaelsen and Robert H. Black, "Building Learning Teams: The Key to Harnessing the Power of Small Groups in Higher Education," *Growth Partners,* 1994.

1 COMMUNICATION IN GROUPS AND TEAMS

STRAITJACKETS OR GLASS SLIPPERS?

As the twentieth century drew to a close, workplace communication underwent a disorienting shift: Just as organizations began to embrace and to implement teams as the prescription for almost every illness, Internet technology exploded, online usage grew at a staggering pace, and before you could say "dot.com," the word *team* became part of America's business lexicon.

Work groups are an indisputable Twenty-First Century necessity for most of us, one likely to continue to dominate organizational life as industries, businesses, organizations, institutions, and communities adapt to a dramatically evolving global marketplace. In this more complex world, with increasing societal and community demands, individuals still need group systems to function effectively and to support everyday activities.

With e-commerce as the value driver of the new economy, technology has brought sudden, sweeping changes to the ways we communicate in businesses, with one another, and within teams. Unsurprisingly, these changes have also encouraged a growing tendency to question not only our extensive use of teams in the workplace but also our basic assumptions about effective communication strategies. As dissatisfaction gradually set in with our existing vocabulary to explain, describe, and implement those strategies, two predictable but opposing reactions have emerged in the literature of the new economy: first, unfamiliar, exotic terms that distort, belabor, or reinvent words; and second, rising attention-deficit cases toward the whole subject. Even to the casual observer, evidence quickly emerged that e-commerce has produced disturbing results regarding individual and organizational communication competencies: poor interpersonal skills, decaying written skills, a deliberate disregard or contempt for standard rules, an unwillingness to listen, and a general lack of nonverbal awareness.

Gartner Group predicts that up to 60 percent of consumer dot.coms formed between 1997 and 2000 will be dead by 2005.[1] Why should any of this concern managers? In the first wake of the dot.com surge, difficulties with interpersonal skills surfaced. A workforce more interactive with desktops and devices than with co-workers has trouble connecting with clients or reconnecting established relationships. The need to develop and to practice interpersonal communication created a stampede toward workshops, retreats, and training sessions to refresh underused, or perhaps never fully realized, skills. The imperative to go online—whether to answer your e-mail or to check your stocks—as the first order of daily activity is a powerful, insular, and addictive inducement to disconnect from others. The repetitive, mechanistic familiarity of the routine is comforting, nonthreatening, and somewhat seductive: Many of us would *rather* begin the day interacting with the computer than with people. As an eye-opener, going online requires no physical energy, no expression or enthusiasm (nonverbal communication), no pain (unless checking stocks), and, of course, no listening. For some it is as necessary as that first cup of coffee.

Small wonder, then, that in spite of accepting assignments to an increasing number of teams, managers often willingly seek refuge in electronic communication and online problem solving rather than face another time-consuming, frustrating, or enraging team meeting with humans. With performance expectations always rising and often elusive and the need for speed paramount, management styles reflect the sad reality of interpersonal skills caught in a crossfire of technology, looming deadlines, and stress.

Technological tremors also course through written communication. If speed is the front line of commerce, effective written communication is usually the first casualty. Even if managers know better, they often run for shortcuts out of self-, or team, preservation: "We've got no time for this. Just get it done." Then the familiar, ringing refrain swells as the inevitable payback comes: "We have a communication problem."

The technologies of the Twenty-First Century have enabled us to communicate faster; now we can confuse, insult, and offend people across the globe as fast as we can hit the Send or Reply buttons. Instant messaging has resulted in instant reactions and spontaneous solutions without adequate reflection or analysis. Excessive reliance on e-mail has encouraged ineffectual communication habits such as single drafts, lack of organization, casual regard for the conventions of grammar and mechanics, acronymic writing and personal shorthand, abrupt and unconsidered responses, and careless reading. Core communication skills across the board, in fact, have declined relative to dependency on software to format, create, and correct written documents. Everyone is susceptible to the temptation to value pace over accuracy. We often communicate as if we were selling commodities in the Chicago Mercantile Exchange and the market closes in five minutes. "No time—no time! Buy! . . . no, . . . sell, . . . no, . . . send!"

Technology has not only accelerated the way we communicate but has actually transformed the languages and symbols we use to do it. Some languages and vocabularies are more malleable than others, and business communication probably best indicates that fluidity and suppleness. The number of new words, pseudo-words, and acronyms added to our daily interaction not only increases the distance between us but also the frequency of our misunderstandings. Related aftershocks also reverberate clearly around the world as we readily communicate across borders and across languages without critical preparation for the linguistic, cultural, and contextual complexities of transferring meaning. One imprudent sound bite can inflict misunderstanding and pain, if not unwelcome, global scrutiny.

New applications for old terms can cause trouble that occasionally courts must sort out. *Temp,* for example, used to mean a temporary worker who was either free-lance or assigned to a company from an employment agency for up to six months. Since such employees were not committed to the company over the long term, the company's attitude was traditionally impersonal and uncommitted. Today, however, temporary workers—those not designated as permanent employees—provide a wide range of services and functions for companies and have become part of the structure if not the actual business plan. Distinctions between the empowered, anointed, and otherwise privileged inner group of workers and temps is significant, while the length of time employed may no longer be the defining feature. Microsoft, for example, reached a $97 million settlement in March 2001 with a group of temporary workers who had filed a federal lawsuit challenging its employment practices. Microsoft had steadily employed some of these temps as long as fourteen years.[3]

Finally, today we are more often and more easily confused because of the volume of information available to and imposed upon us. We read, and sometimes respond, with less accuracy because we have less certainty. Overnight, while we sleep, messages keep coming—an endless stream of e-mail (which we learned to put in folders to answer later), a barrage of advertisements, commercials, and phone solicitations, and fast-talking experts who used enough hot industry jargon to convince us that we needed them as translators. Picture the following: a financial analyst explaining diversification to a warehouse loader; a product-unit manager at Oracle recommending hardware specifications to a dentist; or an IT support technician providing help to a seventy-year-old first-time user. Remember the 3Com commercial advocating simpler networking?

> *You'll need to open several firewall ports and modify the packet filtering on the 4500 router using IOS so your extranets can communicate with our e-servers over the 6 meg fractional T3 line . . . still with me?*

Amid the disorienting jargon, the misinformation, the scams, the spams, and the fraudulent, invasive, and illegal web messages, we're naturally a little confused, a little less trusting, a little more cynical, and a little more impatient. Communicating complex information to different kinds of listeners is one of the most challenging responsibilities managers and teams face, and few seem to know or agree on the right way to do it.

Team Quote ▼

The people who get the biggest rewards seem to operate with a very different set of skills than academics. Entrepreneurs move fast; in the academic world speed is considered a sign of superficiality. "It took me just three months to write my book on the French Revolution," to professors, signals a book not worth reading. Entrepreneurs take a lot of risk, looking to the prospect of gain; academics are famously cautious, calculating what they stand to lose. Entrepreneurs are gregarious and typically have the capacity to build teams and motivate others. These qualities are rare in the academic world, where achievement is usually the result of individual excellence.

— Dinesh D'Souza[4] ▲

In hard times, the soft stuff is particularly important because the impact of a slow economy takes its toll: Good managers often abandon good communication strategies out of sheer panic.

After all, it is difficult to move gracefully toward the exit when your pants are on fire. However, when major mistakes appear repeatedly as reports on global news networks, it's more difficult to pretend no one is watching.

The Ford Explorer/Firestone tire crisis seems to be a good example of a bad communication strategy. First both companies denied the problems, then blamed the customers, then blamed the weather, then one particular tire, then only one plant, then one another, then . . . we stopped listening. This communication blunder was played out nightly on the evening news. Microsoft, of course, is the twenty-first century version of Standard Oil's grand monopoly of the last century. Featured in editorials, cartoons, news, and business reports more often than any other U.S. corporation, the company holds a dominant share of consumers' attention largely because of its coverage in various media. Some viewers have long memories. General Motors Corporation lost more than $2.2 billion trying to win a labor struggle with the United Auto Workers Union in the late 1990s. Threats, intimidation, walkouts, lockouts, and inflexible positions have characterized their relationship over the years. "GM ought to have learned from this strike that it can't win labor showdowns. They've had 24 strikes since 1990, and it hasn't solved anything."[5]

Not so long ago, e-mail guidelines precluded delivering bad news, particularly performance appraisals, firings, personal criticisms, or poor investment news online. In the flurry of dot.com crashes, however, such news became standard operating procedure rather more typical than unusual. Recent economic events are replete with examples, but one of the most startling illustrations is Net-tel, a D.C.-based telecom provider, that espoused creating a different kind of workplace, asking employees to "treat others as you want to be treated" and to "maintain a sense of humanity and humor."[6] Suddenly, on October 23, 2000, the company sought liquidation under Chapter 7 of the federal bankruptcy code. Unfortunately, 300 employees learned about it through a terse e-mail from CEO James Kenefick, who wrote, "It is time to pack up your personal items and move on in life."[7] The backlash from one group of employees stunned Kenefick, who they regarded as an "arrogant and disengaged" CEO: Engineers and customer support representatives destroyed $100,000 worth of network routing equipment, in addition to videotaping equipment, PCs, faxes, and printers.[8]

Even in established, high-performing, and more successful organizations, though, increasingly ineffective communicators, collected into teams, pushed for time, and stressed out by more pressing concerns, often display debilities quickly, creating difficulties that grow exponentially if not managed and monitored closely. Meaning becomes lost, distorted, and sometimes garbled in the pace of the work, the rush to proceed at all costs ("After all, we're a business."), and the relentless pressure to outdistance competitors regardless of whether we really understand what we are doing and why. Most of the time, we understand the how, but unless we understand the why (all too often a procedural casualty), we have not transferred meaning to one another. Web-based management in particular requires teams of individuals who can sort, interpret, and synthesize information in order to stay ahead of the disclosure curve. We have also become increasingly adept at talking over and past one another while giving a convincing impression that we are listening.

We all know that communication skills remain as the number one competency most needed in the workplace today for most organizations; that need is unlikely to change anytime soon, especially since poor skills are a primary cause of team failure.[9] Trouble is, the range of skills involved in demonstrating that competency extends ever steadily outward; moreover, competing pressures to perform these skills more quickly and more accurately accelerate the confusion and come with higher risks.

WHEN ARE TEAMS APPROPRIATE?

Using teams only when appropriate is one of the initial ways managers can communicate well.[10] Managers who ignore the need to legitimize or to communicate the need for a team miss an important opportunity to establish effective (team communication) **TeamComm** strategies at the outset. Simply put, **TeamComm** is a protocol: the rules of communication for managing the work of the team. Applying the **TeamComm** system establishes good communication practices among team members; manages conflict during the work processes; and provides a framework for team members to establish clear values, procedures, and strategies. Understanding the reasons for lackluster team performance is especially difficult later if members never understand or accept the need for a team. If managers communicate a clear, balanced, and realistic set of expectations, teams have a much better chance at success.

Companies continue to search for innovative and foolproof ways to identify, recruit, develop, retain, and reward managers, employees, and teams with excellent communication skills. But the need to create new business plans, to define new models, to navigate new territories, to rebuild credibility, to manage crises, to create value for themselves and others, or to assuage customers, investors, shareholders, and even disgruntled employees can create overwhelming pressures. Too often, the behavior seems to mirror the attitude that "Something has to give. If you can't keep up, get out of the way." If pace is paramount, then the inevitable result is acceleration. So far, though, no one has managed to adjust human capacities to be in line with new capabilities. We do not create meaning any faster simply because we can deliver the messages sooner.

In the rush to respond to a continually expanding landscape, businesses and teams can regain control and composure by following a few simple rules:

- Manage the technology, or it will manage you.
- Use a systematic approach to organizational and personal communication.
- Customize the procedures and tailor them for your people.

Using a comprehensive, customized approach to communication not only makes sense in the short run, it saves time, energy, and resources in the end. If technology has ultimately provided the most frequent explanation for poor skills (and, therefore, a guilt-free excuse for why messages fail), it has also provided powerful enhancements to those skills. The key lies in using technology to enhance, rather than to control, our communication. Businesses (even start-ups) that connect strategic advantage and communication with appropriate emphases on products, services, and technology will survive any economy. Such an enhancement can yield powerful results for consumers, shareholders, and constituents who understand all too well that straitjackets are one-size-fits-all; but the glass slipper fit only one foot.

Team Quote ▼

As important as it is for information on the Internet to be filtered, personalized, and intelligent, it is dramatically more so on wireless devices.

— Brad Silverberg, former head of Microsoft's Windows business and current CEO and Chairman of Ignition[11] ▲

NEW APPROACHES FOR OLD HANDS

Most of us understand and accept that teams are not merely a workplace reality for the twenty-first century but also a necessity. If conflict is an inevitable part of that necessity, teams can function as both a cause and a cure. Still, as the single most efficient organizational tool for accomplishing work previously delegated to individuals, teams allow managers to define work performance expectations through departments, divisions, or units. Few have failed to notice that, as technology has escalated performance standards, workloads, and pace, the team approach has rapidly become the norm by which organizations deliver products, measure customer satisfaction, and forecast growth.

Teams also seem to pose the most effective response to organizational change, just as groups in Paleolithic society formed the strongest unit against the forces of the natural world. As Jessica Lipnack and Jeffrey Stamps point out, "When you think back to the beginning of human work, hunting and gathering happened in small bands of family groups. Those were the first teams. Through the cycle of seasons, small groups would come together into larger family kinship networks, share the harvest, and go off in individual groups again when food got scarce."[12] Since most expert predictions indicate that understanding and adapting to change is the one future constant for organizational success, managers must still learn to adapt the tools available to the group's needs. That may mean using new ways to describe ancient methods or adapting current systems to reflect evolving environments. At the very least, it requires constant vigilance. The more synchronized businesses are with the climate and challenges of change, the more likely their survival and profitability.

Implementation of teams in the workplace—sometimes indiscriminately—has also created new attitudes for workers, shifting in the last few years from "Will this be a team effort?" to "*Another* team?" Little wonder, then, that many businesses, organizations, corporations, and institutions have reported mixed results on the use of teams. The latest backlash for some of us is to ask for a return to the individualistic, competitive methods of an earlier era. This preference for a preteam culture may just signal a reaction to a more volatile and uncertain economy or, in fact, a natural instinct to reject collective wisdom in favor of self-reliance.

What we have here is a failure to communicate.
— Strother Martin, in *Cool Hand Luke* ▲

In spite of numerous research studies, reports, and other information currently available on managing teams and improving team practices, confusion persists about the processes involved, as does resistance to team efforts, often by jaded workers suspicious about the collective wisdom of using teams, or by students overloaded with too many team projects. Think about it, though. Do we really want to encourage a return to "my way or the highway" thinking? Do we just throw out the lessons learned over the course of a decade of unprecedented economic growth through team efforts?

One response managers may choose is to counter resistance to teamwork through fresh approaches. If change is the one constant in the workplace, the single constant of productive team performance is clear, accurate, and effective communication among members. With management education only a hundred years old, skilled communicators bring a respect for that fairly recent past while incorporating innovative methods. They encourage entrepreneurial, high-risk activities while supporting and reinforcing good team skills already learned. The two styles are different means serving the same end.

<table>
<tr><td>Team Quote ▼</td></tr>
</table>

Team-building is hard when the word "delisting" is in the air and the office is filled with empty desks and the ghosts of former colleagues. It's time now for bold countermeasures. . . . Let's go back to the original corporate raiders. . . . When these guys dealt with headhunters, it was never a war of dueling cell phones. Actual heads were involved. Rather than cushy resort hotels or conference centers, executives need to take their employees to decommissioned army barracks. Nothing like showering together to break down inhibitions. . . .

Imagine for a moment the evaluation session . . . in close combat, aim for the eyeballs and the groin; there is no such thing as a fair fight. Aren't employees who trust no one and attack without warning what the modern CEO is really looking for? As for "goals," those would be even easier. "Penetrate, infiltrate, eliminate." Catchy, accurate, and chantable. If you're the only team left standing, team-building gets real easy.

— Jon Carroll, *Not Another Team-Building Exercise*[13] ▲

Resistance to the use of teams arises from personal experience with them and their widespread use in almost every sector of business, industry, education, technology, human relations, and social services. Also, overuse of the term itself for any work done by more than one person often brings people together under a false assumption: that each member brings the same understanding, attitudes, and expertise to the team. Using a team reframes the organization's workplace behavior and strategies, but unless managers are able to explain why a team is necessary for the effort and how the team's work connects to the work of others', communication problems will start even before the team is formed.

While our assumptions about the workplace may change as quickly as new markets open overseas, teams will continue to evolve as the most effective means of completing multiple tasks simultaneously. If a solid foundation for appropriate communication strategies is in place *before* a team starts its work, fewer cracks are likely to appear as the group settles into its tasks.

TeamComm strategies, while drawing on some familiar individual communication skills, require a broader view of competencies, perspectives, behavior, and processes. In short, being an effective communicator means being versatile and flexible while managing ideas, strategies, and people. Teams composed of members with strong skills and training across the board obviously have more inner resources to pull from than teams without. Cross-functional teams composed of individuals with clearly identified functional skills but who lack interactive or interpersonal expertise are more likely to have a polarizing team experience. Individuals with superior critical thinking skills, for example, and who can communicate their ideas in multiple ways simply have more options. Verbal, nonverbal, visual, and conceptual skills can make the difference between a thought that dies in the air or an idea that can reshape teams, organizations, and commerce.

KINDS OF TEAMS

Whether defined as a working group, a real or performing team, a project team, a pseudo-team, an executive management team, a high-performance team, a leader-led team, a consensus group, a task force, or a committee, members form an eclectic. As such, they need and want clear communication processes. While the specific applications of those processes depend on the kind of team formed, as well as on the organization in which it does its work, the communication framework determines whether the group will function well as a team. The framework the team adopts must be flexible enough to serve the needs specifically mandated by the makeup of the team, and the team must recognize and respect that flexibility.

In rethinking teams here, we can classify them into four types, based on task definition: project teams, strategic teams (sometimes called top management teams), research teams, and developmental teams. Such teams may be physical or virtual, homogeneous or cross-functional. The following distinctions will serve as a guide as you form and build teams, and as you evaluate teamwork:

Project team: two or more people who temporarily share time-defined goals and mandates specifically tied to a product, an event, or an activity.

Strategic team: two or more people with shared goals for the organization's internal processes, objectives, or overall strategies and with shared responsibility for the organization's success.

Research team: two or more people united by their mutual goals and interests through independent pursuits and collaborative results.

Developmental team: two or more people who perform collaborative, interdependent activities based on shared mutual goals.

The labels, in fact, are less important than the activities these teams perform. Since the activities may take place in physical or electronic settings, any of these teams may also be virtual as well. TeamComm applies to many different groups and the name distinctions help only insofar as they serve teams in designing appropriate individual—or customized—TeamComm strategies, whether reaching across time and space or across the table.

All of these can improve team communication by focusing on team assessments, team analysis, documentation, and evaluation. More enduringly, TeamComm can make the experience rewarding, increase the team's achievements, and improve future teamwork. A team formed or built by a manager/leader who regards communication strategies as the cornerstone of the team's success will ensure that it has the necessary resources. Without those, a team may muddle through, meet deadlines, or get a product to market, but associate such negativity with teamwork that it never reaches its full, collaborative potential. When that happens (as it often does), these members bring destructive, and sometimes fatal, attitudes to the next project or team effort.

MANAGING COMMUNICATION PROTOCOL

Why is effective communication the determinant of team success?

Those who share an understanding of purpose, identity, context, process, protocol, and collaboration also understand team achievement. They do not need to be told if they hit or missed the mark—they know it. Those who watched the 1999 Women's World Cup Soccer Final, the largest crowd ever to attend such an event, witnessed a highly trained, collaborative team in action. As if a system projected in 3-D animation, the team modeled synergistic action as a single unit. Each player moved like an extension of the other, achieving higher levels of play with every touch and challenge. *That* team, and that performance in particular, inspired unprecedented, global media attention, articles, and at least two books to date. Professional sports—male or female—had never seen anything like it.

Team Quote ▼

It's a shared vision of who we are.
— Michelle Akers, U.S. Women's Soccer
Team, 1999 World Cup Champions[15] ▲

Managers more often receive evaluations and rewards for individual effort than for team success. In spite of all the team training over the past decade, managers trust their instincts for effective work processes, which originate with individual style, motivation, and educational experiences. If they have been successful in their educational, professional, or experiential programs with the single leader approach,[16] the instinct will be to apply this same style to successive team situations. If, however, they have achieved greater success with collaborative approaches either through their educational programs or in the workplace, then they may assume that this strategy is always appropriate for group work. Managers tend to go with their gut reaction, using familiar, generalized methods, rather than take time to rethink, relearn, or reinvent strategies.

Moreover, when managers attempt to manage other managers, conflicting styles can collide, resulting in a struggle for power and resources. Clashing ideas can signal the first whiffs of smoke for what later develops into flaming confrontation if each manager is heavily invested in the deeply held (but unspoken) belief that teamwork is a sanctioned way of assuming dominance over a group. While often unexpressed, this attitude interferes not only with the team's outcomes but also with its ability to communicate about what those outcomes should be. Regardless of the attitudes held, open, clear confrontation methods and trust for both individual and collective wisdom are essential for building an effective team. If members do not own a shared vision of who they are, what the goals are, what processes they will use, what resources they hold, and how they will measure success, they will never be a team.

USING A SYSTEMS APPROACH TO TEAM COMMUNICATION

Managing teams well means caring about and caring for the people and processes involved. As analysts Katzenbach and Smith have pointed out, the desire to *be* a team is not enough.[18] In the last decade, the team literature has stressed learning to work cooperatively, developing trust, and understanding collaboration, but the increasingly complex challenges facing teams still outpace our ability to implement changes in our work systems to respond accordingly.

Team Quote ▼

Teamwork is a lot of people doing what I say.
— Citrix Corp. Marketing Executive [17] ▲

While some still hold the view—either privately or openly—that the dominant, ranking leader dictates goals and activities, most managers have learned that an open process enhances group interaction, dynamics, decision making, and performance results. Desire does not translate magically into achievement. If the group coalesces primarily around the idea of becoming a team but neglects strategy, process, refinements, feedback, regrouping, and reflection, the group will remain . . . just a group.

Many have pointed to systems thinking as a key to effective management, leadership, and communication, while gently and succinctly reminding us that a **system** is simply "the method by which you achieve results."[19] By using a systems approach to managing team communication, then, we might ask a few questions:

- What skills or competencies do we/I have/need?
- What skills and processes do we need in this effort?
- What strengths/weaknesses do we/I bring to the team?
- How will we measure success?
- What resources do we have/need to go forward?
- How will we accomplish the work?

Embracing the evolving applications of teamwork means adopting a communication strategy as malleable as the team concept itself. But, since learning new strategies merely for the sake of continual learning rarely works, only implementation, experimentation, adaptation, and refinement make a strategy useful. TeamComm strategies can assist teams in becoming synergistic, then, only if teams regard communication as a system central to their formal work. By using a specific method, exploring the model, and applying a framework *before* the functional work begins, teams can leverage their abilities to anticipate and overcome challenges.

APPLYING THE TEAMCOMM MODEL

The model shown in Figure 1 represents TeamComm processes at five levels: self, group, institution, culture, and technology. Concentric circles extend the context of communication issues and considerations, but the basic analytical process that teams use is the same at all five levels.

Information increases at each level, adding to the group's understanding of required abilities to address communication complexities. To frame it as a process involves an interconnected series of steps: assessment, analysis, documentation, implementation, and evaluation.

Teams skilled in multiple tasks and processes can operate on as many levels as are applicable to their context, as long as they treat the levels sequentially. The framework focuses the team on its fundamental target: what it has, what it needs, and how to get where it wants to go.

We know that communication is a problem, but the company is not going to discuss it with the employees.
— AT&T Long Lines Division Manager[20] ▲

Figure 1   A Systems Model for TeamComm

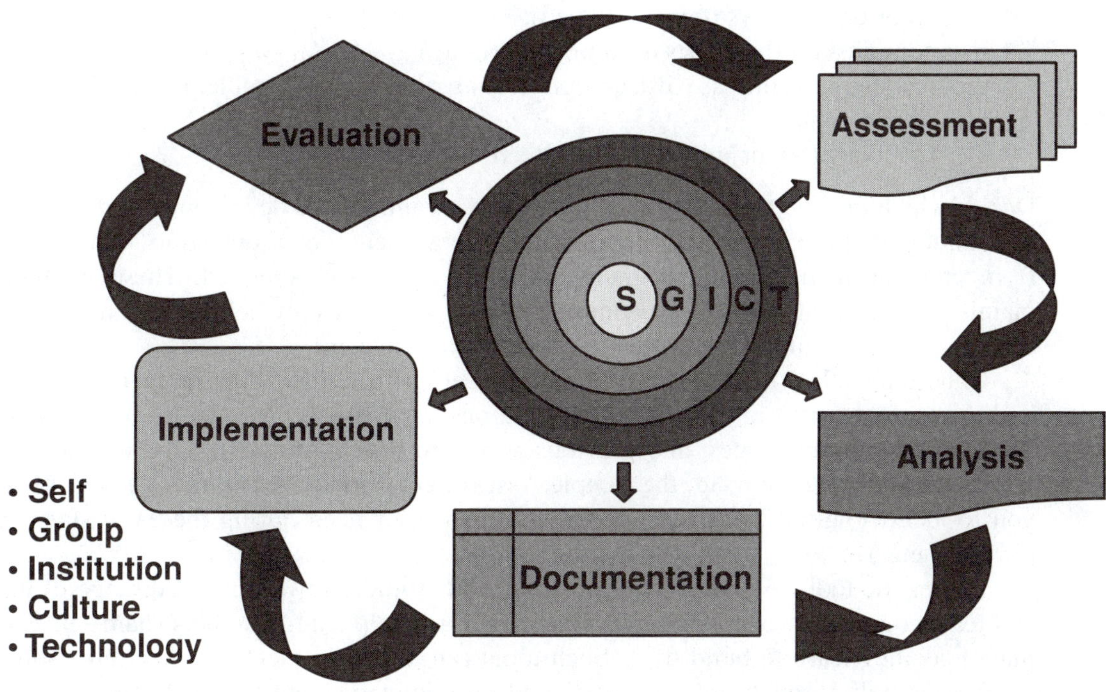

SELF-ASSESSMENT

Good TeamComm begins with assessing each team member's individual communication skills. Such self-analysis helps each member determine honestly and objectively what each can and will offer the group. Strategically, it is an essential first step in building a safe climate to express ideas, doubts, reservations, misapprehensions, appraisals, and praise. Most managers, particularly those with substantial leadership responsibilities, believe that they are good communicators, but unless each member has an accurate and current self-image, the team composite will be distorted. Skill sets change more quickly these days, as do others' perceptions of those skills. As Steven Berglas warns, "The essence of managing in the Information Age will be in accepting that all knowledge workers, over time, will shed skill sets and develop new ones, just as a reptile sheds skin."[21]

Since it can be difficult to base self-analyses on subjective impressions alone, members and teams can document their assessments with performance appraisals, feedback, annual report evaluations, certifications, awards, and other support. However, members should take care to assess skills based on knowledge and belief (trust). A team member who has received glowing feedback on outcomes that she or he was only tangentially involved with producing or that were largely in place before that member joined the project would not only practice self-deception in recording such successes but also team deception. Misleading team members about individual skills is singularly unwise; by the time the team discovers the truth, it may be too late to correct assumptions or needed resources.

Other assessment methods include:

- diagnostic tools (team or company designed);
- professionally designed instruments;
- self-profiles (psychological tests, biographies, or journals);
- written or oral surveys (team designed);
- lists compiled on flip charts (oral brainstorming);
- group consensus software distribution (team brainstorming; problem-identification; voting procedures); and
- synchronous or asynchronous data collection.

Decide which method to use based on team needs, training, and development information available through the company's human resources department, communications center, or perhaps from previous management programs members may have attended. These methods differ mainly in format but they share a common goal: to access deeply held beliefs, attitudes, values, or opinions that would help members perform well as a team.

Choose a method to assess each team member's skills, depending on members' familiarity with one another, trust in each others' evaluations, tenure with the organization, background or functional area, preferences, and previous access to this information. One way to gather this information is to use or adapt the sample Assessment Forms. (**Assessment Form #1** will help you to identify initial areas of concern, confidence, or need during the early stages of team development.)

Diagnostic tools to identify various skills and attitudes toward a broad range of individual and team competencies are widely available and can help team members share sensitive information as they learn to build trust. Such tools can also help members determine self-profiles more accurately through objective tests and questionnaires and thus help teams identify and establish a group picture. Whether designed by the team, the company, or professional consultants,

ASSESSMENT FORM #1
Communication Skills Self-Assessment

Use the following chart to assess your current communication proficiency based on a scale of 1 to 5.

Scale:
5 – I am completely confident in my ability.
4 – I am confident in my ability.
3 – I am somewhat confident in my ability.
2 – I am confident that I could improve my ability.
1 – I am not confident in my ability.

Skill	1	2	3	4	5	Include examples or a specific context where appropriate.
Written Work:						
E-mail						
Reports						
Other						
Change Communication (policies, procedures, etc.)						
Collaboration						
Diversity Skills						
Listening Skills						
Media Communication						
Negotiation Experience						
Nonverbal Skills						
Performance Evaluations/ Feedback						
Team Training or Group Process Skills						

ASSESSMENT FORM #1
Communication Skills Self-Assessment

INDIVIDUAL ACTION PLAN:
Improving Communication Skills

Create an action plan to address your top priorities.

Targeted Skill	1.	2.	3.
Improvement Strategy(ies)			
Current Proficiency			
Desired Outcome			
Date Started			
Progress Level: Scale 1–5			
Date Measured			

however, assessment methods and instruments can measure a wide range of managerial skills. A few of the better known instruments include Kolb's Model of Experiential Learning, Myers/Briggs Type Inventory®, Keirsey Temperament Sorter®, and DISC tools (behavioral style indicators).[22] Other commercially available tools also measure listening skills, adaptability to change, leadership styles, assertiveness levels, conflict views, work environment preferences, negotiation skills, and attitudes toward diversity.

TEAM COMPETENCIES AND SKILLS

Following the individual self-assessments, meet with your team members to identify collective strengths and weaknesses—defining what those are and why they are important for this effort— through open discussion to synthesize team results.

This time the members continue the needs assessment from a team perspective by comparing data gathered from the self-assessments about skills, attitudes, team views, strengths, weaknesses, differences in styles and experiences, and so on. Openness about strengths and weaknesses is easier here if the initial self-assessment process has been thorough and objective. Unless a climate of trust exists, your team may be reluctant to share personal views or self-critical information.

Some teams, in fact, prefer to have a facilitator guide them through this process of skill identification and type analyses and are more comfortable if an outsider profiles the group as, for example, largely intuitive types and only one member with analytical skills. If, however, all the members seem to be pragmatists but the project effort will require highly creative and innovative work, the team may want either to rethink its composition or to target certain aspects of the project for advisory support.

Pinpointing areas for adjustment, development, or projected need is a critical step in these early stages. None of us likes to admit weaknesses, even if they may be obvious to others, but collective wisdom is usually more convincing than one person's opinion. For example, if the project performance will involve mediation skills and one member has no training or experience with conflict management, arbitration, or confrontation methods, this might signal a priority for an individual action plan. Unless that member is at least comfortable with the language and concepts involved, he or she will find it difficult to connect with team discussions of these issues. If the team identifies this as a critical need, that member might more easily recognize that certification in mediation skills or significant training in dispute resolution would improve the overall team effort.

Analyzing team skills is much easier and more accurate *after* initial self-assessments. Members may consciously or unconsciously adjust their own assessments in the context of the larger team results. Similarly, one who values strong leadership may be poles apart from someone else who also values strong leadership but defines it differently. Ironically, it's not uncommon for teams to have initial conflict over their attitudes *toward* conflict and whether they define it positively or negatively.

More important, members may now also adjust their perceptions about the team's strengths and weaknesses. Members may disagree about what strengths they have because they do not agree on what signifies strength. A member who identifies taking risks as a strength may be at odds with a member who is risk-averse.

TEAM RESOURCES

Once the team reaches an understanding of its current skills and strengths, it can use the assessments to identify resources available to support the team or individual members in their efforts.

Having already outlined individual strengths and weaknesses also helps teams now extend the inventory of connections, contacts, databases, programs, and other systems to provide a roadmap for next steps. For uncharted territory ("None of us has ever tried this before!"), such inventories go a long way in building confidence in the team's ability to deliver expected outcomes.

Similarly, if gaping holes become obvious, identify resources early to supplement the effort.

- What other perspectives do we need for this project?
- Is additional training necessary?
- Are effective coaches and mentors available?
- Are additional funds necessary? If so, what are the open avenues for assistance?
- Are there gaps in experience or understanding, learning, or expertise?
- Will we need consultants or knowledge managers to identify these?
- Are there models or prototypes available?
- What other kinds of support are needed to accomplish the goal(s)?
- What contingency plans do we need?
- How would changes in the market/industry/climate affect these resources?
- Is the organization set up to support our recommendations?

Recording the competency areas, needs, and resources (**Assessment Form #2**) can help teams formally plan strategy and set expectations. If the team sets unrealistic goals, or lacks the skills or resources to meet those targets, clearly it heads for disappointment. Recognizing the gaps may not be difficult, but admitting that they present major barriers is. The more thoroughly a team analyzes its position and its needs, the more accurate a picture the team will have of its future.

ORGANIZATIONAL ASSESSMENT

The organizational or **institutional context** involves mission, ideology, attitudes, behavior, and habits. How does the team's charge fit in the company's organizational strategy? Is the team's work a priority? Does management view its work as supplementary, experimental, or marginal? How have organizational expectations affected previous team efforts? How have these teams traditionally been recognized, rewarded, or compensated? Within organizational norms, where does this team fit? Is the team composed of people from one department or division or from throughout the company? Would this team represent a departure, an innovative development, a retrospective return, or a disguised attempt to hand down top management's directives in a more palatable way?

Team Quote ▼

You can't say, "teams work because of this" or "teams don't work because of that"—because it depends. But if you're looking for one quality that most good teams share . . . it's the culture of the company in which the team exists. People from different parts of a company are going to have disparate styles, expectations, and reward systems. The best teams have leaders who recognize those differences.

— Martha Rogers, Partner, Peppers and Rogers Group[23] ▲

ASSESSMENT FORM #2
Team Competencies and Skills

Rank the following team needs on a scale of 1 to 5.

Scale:
5 – High
3 – Moderate
1 – Low

Team Competency	Need	Problem Description	Resources	Source of Data	Recommended Action or Strategy
Facilitation					
Communication					
Functional Expertise					
Project Design Negotiation					
Research and Assessment					
Project Development					
Conflict					
Media Relations					

Teams sometimes assume that all internal mechanisms are support networks, but a team that understands its own history is less likely to discover unpleasant surprises or to repeat the same mistakes. For a highly public example, we need look no further than Firestone. Public relations representatives dealing with the defective tire fiasco presented a different explanation weekly about the reasons for quality failures. Quality control teams were effectively isolated from the decade-old problem with the Explorer until the media uncovered internal documents at both Firestone and Ford Motor Company. Further disclosures continue to reveal details as the investigation continues, while corrective measures to assuage a nonbelieving customer base may take years. The most recent communication strategy John Lampe used was the slogan, "Your safety is our priority." While time and the markets will tell whether this message proves believable, early indications are not promising.

When an organization puts a team in place, it must also clarify how the team's work fits with larger core business and whether or not the organization is set up to be responsive to that work. Rather than viewing any team as an isolated, independent task group that provides data and outcomes to the company, managers should carefully analyze how the company's organizational structure connects to the team. Teams are often stymied by the cold reality that management views their efforts as creating and implementing changes in policy or production that depends on internal organizational restructuring, as well.

Organizations can determine the robustness of a team and save valuable time by using TeamComm assessments to form teams, ensuring an appropriate balance or compatibility of skills but also providing valuable documentation to members once the teams are in place (**Assessment Form #3**).

CULTURAL ASSESSMENT

Widening the lens another notch, TeamComm explores culture—both internal and external to the team. Apart from the organization's policies and routines are cultural assumptions, behaviors, and attitudes that may or may not be obvious. What access does the team have to top management or to key stakeholders? Does the team have direct access to company leadership? Are there power distance issues within the company or among members of the team that would preclude the team's achieving its goals and objectives? Would certain forces within the company like to see the team fail? For members new to the organization, this provides valuable background not easily obtained otherwise.

Beyond the organizational climate lies the global context: How many cultures will this effort represent or affect? What others comprise the organization's constituents? How central is an understanding of cross-cultural communication to our work? Does the work require a multiple lens or a single focus? Does this effort represent our mission at its broadest scope, at its most narrow, or at some other point (**Assessment Form #4**)?

ASSESSMENT FORM #3
Team Organizational Context

Rank each organizational support area according to the following scale.

Scale:
5 – High
4 – Above average
3 – Moderate
2 – Below average
1 – Low

Context Area	Individual Rank	Team Rank	Recommendations
Human Resources			
Material Resources			
Organizational Structure			
Performance Review Measures and Benchmarking			
Access to Leadership			
External Resources (availability of):			
Company Alliances			
Outsourcing			
Coaches or Mentors			
Consultants			
Leadership within Industry			

Respond to the following questions within the context of your company or organization.

What company attitudes are in place to support this team?

What company attitudes are potentially detrimental to this effort?

What company behaviors can contribute to our efforts (networks, formal or informal work groups, interorganizational alliances, community involvement)?

What company behaviors might be detrimental?

What core values are directly connected to our mission?

How does the company view our project/efforts?

With what multiple identities in our company does our mission connect?

What other perspectives do we need to consider for our customers/constituents?

What are the potential costs/benefits of these?

What global cultures does our project or effort affect?

Identify any potential advantages and disadvantages these have on our planning.

What potential changes in market conditions are likely to affect our work before completion?

What potential changes in industry climate would affect our resources or outcomes?

DELIVERY TECHNOLOGY ASSESSMENT

Finally, TeamComm strategies directly emerge from the **technology** (the message delivery medium), the means through which the communication takes place.

- What conditions do we need to consider that will affect our communication methods?
- Will our team mainly comprise independently directed efforts, with occasional group discussions?
- What methods will we use to communicate what kinds of information?
- Will this be a virtual team with access to groupware and videoconferencing?
- What procedures do we need to set for e-mail communication?
- In what ways will we communicate strategy: interpersonally, electronically, or jointly?
- Will consensus or other decision-making software be available should we need it?
- Is individual contact regarding specific questions or information sharing a natural developmental outgrowth or is it likely to be interpreted as collusion?

If, for example, we know that most of our communication will involve multinational, electronic conversations, how do we need to adjust our strategies to avoid miscommunication? Current data indicates that people read more slowly online than on the written page, that plain language cuts reading time from 23% to 17%, and that multicultural teams (more than two members from different cultures) take longer to connect initially and to sort out process issues.[24]

Team Quote ▼

The reason people stay at a company is that it's a great place to work. It's like playing on a great sports team. Really good players want to be around other really good players.

— John Chambers, CEO,
Cisco Systems Inc.[25] ▲

Again, inventories of technology assumptions aid team members in recognizing what tools they will have readily available, as well as identifying needed resources (**Assessment Form #5**). Of course, teams who have worked together over several projects or several years will adjust the use and implementation of the model based on their experiences with one another. If communication problems have been prevalent in the past, it may take these teams longer to overcome their need to recharge themselves and renew their mission. The longer these problems have been in place, the harder they will be to overcome. While some teams set several sessions or retreats to design their operating model, others may need only one. Simply put, teams must consider their unique conditions when setting up communication strategies.

DISCUSSION QUESTIONS

1. What *kind* of team are you a member of?

2. What leadership structures did you consider before choosing one? Why is this structure the best fit for this team?

ASSESSMENT FORM #5
Delivery Technology

Use the following chart to assess your current proficiency on communication technology based on a scale of 1 to 5.

Scale:
5 – High
4 – Above average
3 – Moderate
2 – Below average
1 – Low

Delivery Method	1	2	3	4	5	Comments
E-mail						
Hard Copy						
Phone or Wireless Communication						
Groupware						
Teleconferencing						
Web Delivery						
Fax						
Other						

3. What are the greatest communication challenges you face individually with this team's mission? Under what conditions do you do your best work?

4. How could your team help you with this?

5. What characteristics of e-mail do you find most helpful and most troublesome? Check all that apply.

Asynchronicity	
Tone	
Format	
Style	
Delivery System (servers, technology, etc.)	
Other	

6. What discussion methods would you prefer for team decision making? Check all that apply.

Face-to-Face Meetings	
Q/A Submitted to Group in Advance of Meetings	
Online Discussion Boards	
Group Decision Systems (allowing anonymous postings)	
Other	

ENDNOTES

1. Susan Moran, "Minimum Tax, Maximum Headache," *Business 2.0,* February 6, 2001, 79.
2. Michael J. Mandel and Robert D. Hof, "Rethinking the Internet," *BusinessWeek,* March 26, 2001, 118.
3. Moran, 80–81.
4. D'Souza's comment appears in his article "Lottery of Success," *Business 2.0,* December 12, 2000, 224. [The Editor notes that the article was adapted from D'Souza's recently released book, *The Virtue of Prosperity: Finding Values in an Age of Techno-Affluence* (New York: Free Press, 2000).]
5. A. Bernstein, P. Galuszka, and R. Barker, "What Price Peace? GM Lost a Lot to the UAW, and Labor Relations Are Still Bad," *BusinessWeek,* August 10, 1998, 24–25.
6. Kim Girard, "Return of the Crummy Job," *Business 2.0,* February 6, 2001, 75.
7. Ibid.
8. Ibid.
9. David Ewing, in a brochure announcing the introduction of *Management Communication Quarterly,* Sage Publications, 1997. Anne Donnellon treats the significance of talk in depth in her book *Team Talk: The Power of Language in Team Dynamics* (Boston: Harvard Business School Press, 2000).
10. Most researchers and practitioners agree that using teams is not always an appropriate strategy, particularly if the reasons for doing so are not explicit. See, for example, R. J. Hackman, ed., *Groups That Work (and Those That Don't): Creating Conditions for Effective Teamwork* (San Francisco: Jossey-Bass, 1990).
11. Bill Snyder, "Five Questions with . . . Brad Silverberg, CEO and Chairman of Ignition," *http://www.business2.com/articles,* December 12, 2000.
12. Steven Berglas, *Virtual Teams: People Working Across Boundaries with Technology* (New York: Wiley, 2001), 6.
13. *Business 2.0,* May 15, 2001, 76.
14. *Business 2.0,* December 12, 2000, 97.
15. Mariah Burton Nelson, "Learning What 'Team' Really Means," *Newsweek,* July 19, 1999, 55.
16. See, for example, Jon R. Katzenbach and Douglas Smith, *The Wisdom of Teams: Creating the High-Performance Organization* (New York: HarperCollins, 1993, rpt. 1999), xxii.
17. Quotations online: see *http://www.bartleby.com.* This quotation has been variously ascribed and repeated. Ascribed to Michael Winner, British film director, "A team effort is a lot of people doing what I say," by Robert Byrne in *1,911 Best Things Anybody Ever Said* (New York: Ballantine, 1988), 356.
18. Katzenbach and Smith, xvii.
19. Peter Scholtes, *The Leader's Handbook* (New York: McGraw-Hill, 1998), 23.
20. Quotations online.
21. Berglas, 99.
22. See Appendix A for information on these and other resources.
23. Regina Maruca, "What Makes Teams Work?" *Fast Company,* November 2000, *http://pf.fastcompany.com/online/40/one.html.*
24. See James Suchan and Robert Colucci, "An Analysis of Communication Efficiency between High-Impact and Bureaucratic Written Communication," *Management Communication Quarterly,* 2 (May 1989): 454–484.
25. John A. Byrne, "Visionary vs. Visionary," *BusinessWeek,* August 28, 2000, 212.

2 TEAMCOMM PERFORMANCE STRATEGIES

PLANNING TEAMCOMM STRATEGIES

The TeamComm framework helps teams navigate common potential hazards so they can focus more efficiently on external forces, shifting demographics, and marketplace strategies. Regardless of what framework teams use or what they call it, the point is this: Teams need a **communication protocol** (rules for managing team communication) that they understand and accept—even if they create their own.

After formation and any preteam activities or readings to prepare members for the transition to the project, a team should begin to address the essential team process questions. These questions will help members think out loud; clear the air about behaviors; and review the basics, such as setting goals and objectives, establishing ground rules, selecting leadership models, planning communication strategies, forming partnerships, and determining evaluation procedures. Let's look at these basic guidelines that transform individual work into group work.

WHAT ARE OUR TEAM GOALS AND OBJECTIVES?

Defining goals can be difficult for some teams if they confuse desired results with measurable outcomes: What will indicate team success? And how do teams know when they get there? Sometimes teams only recognize when they don't.

If the primary goal is to perform well (or language equally general), the outcomes (quantifiable products) will be fuzzy both to the team and the organization. While the connection between goal setting and performance measurement may seem obvious, communicating clearly about that connection is not. Many organizations misidentify short-term activities as outcomes. Gathering market data and designing an improved organizational flowchart are two examples of such activities. Entering three new niche markets identified through data research or increasing online orders and on-time deliveries by 50% while reducing customer complaints by 40% through a new shipment tracking system, however, are goals with measurable outcomes. As Katzenbach and Smith point out, "Unless and until people understand the performance goals that matter, organizations will fall short of meeting the aspirations of their leaders. This is critical for team performance, which is largely dependent upon clear, compelling outcome-based

In the summer of 1999, Hewlett-Packard revealed its plan for the next stage of development in the Internet. Vice President Ann Livermore announced to eager listeners, including shareholders and reporters, that e-speak *would be "a universal language for e-services on the Net." The idea was for unrelated web sites to communicate with each other, delivering a broad range of services to the user.*

A year later, consumers were still in the dark. As one reporter explained, "For all the bravado, e-speak barely registers on the radar screen. What happened? Call it a communication problem. HP never adequately explained what e-speak could do and why anyone would need it." [1] ▲

goals—particularly when such goals distinguish between individual tasks and the collective (joint) work-products that determine real team performance."[2]

Members more concerned with individual performance (promotion, commission, or salary) also affect goal setting. It is a natural reflex for managers and employees alike to be more concerned with individual contributions and measurements because that is the traditional culture business has engrained in them. As members of a team, some are less likely to see a connection between their work and others' or to understand how their work affects group action in the form of inertia, attitudes, and overall achievement. Reactions and criticisms from these disconnected members are typical and predictable:

- "I'm doing my best. If only the other members of the team would pull their weight."
- "I delivered on my end—the foul-up must have occurred down the line."
- "I have to do everything myself."

Over the years, if such reflexes are habitual, some members may consciously or unconsciously keep private, hidden goals:

- "Even if the team doesn't hit a home run, I can still meet my personal targets."
- "We didn't hit our numbers, but it was a good experience for me."

Other teammates may seem to accept or may even *think* they accept the team's mission as paramount because they understand it; but if they cannot express it, or articulate it in a way the team also accepts, they may not fully embrace it.

- "I'll do whatever the team wants."

Such expressions imply support and the speaker may intend to sound helpful, but noncommittal statements such as these also indicate no specific action, interest, or expertise in anything and place the burden of task responsibility on everyone else.

A few members may not recognize that individual perceptions can differ from team solutions:

- "It's pretty clear what we need to do here."

Is that clarity a shared vision? Or is it simply an individual reaction based on perceived need? Needed outcomes, as specified by management, may in fact set minimal (or maximum) expectations: "To decrease customer complaints by 10%." The team's goal, however, may be closer to 30%. Conversely, if management has an unrealistic expectation (80%) and the team bases its target on data indicating attainable projections, the team can more persuasively communicate that message in order to adjust the goals accordingly.

WHAT ARE OUR TEAM GROUND RULES?

Powers of recall are limited, at best, and until someone creates a brain microchip to upgrade our memory capabilities, teams will always have difficulty remembering the same events in the same way. To guard against these glitches in our mental processes, teams need to meet the challenge of recording procedures for how the team will do its work. If teams are specific and calculated about constructing these, reaching consensus on what the procedures are, how the team will carry them out, and how to make adjustments in these if necessary, they can avoid miscommunication or misinterpretation later.

Of course, agreeing to the need for ground rules is quite different from establishing them. And some teams agree in theory to the big picture but do not fully understand or embrace the need for ground rules. Start with the small stuff first, advises Notre Dame Professor James O'Rourke: "If people can agree on at least a few things, experts say, the big issues won't be as difficult."[3]

When the team eventually articulates project objectives, goals, and performance measurements more specifically, it adds to the power the team has in communicating its own management protocol and procedures. Rules of engagement recorded and monitored for basic team activities also keep the team on track and help it mark its progress.

WHAT LEADERSHIP MODEL WILL WE USE?

At the center of team potential is the choice of leadership. If teams determine their own leadership, success rates skyrocket. If leaders are appointed, or if a managing leader supervises but doesn't participate in the process, they will be neither fully integrated nor very effective.

Traditional patterns of leadership usually fall into three models: the leader-led team, the consensus team, or the managed team. Whereas leader-led teams are by far the oldest and most common approach to team leadership, consensus teams are the most flexible in terms of leadership, and managed teams balance management structure with team interdependence. Leadership options depend on team needs, task scope, human resources, due dates, and TeamComm choices. Discussions at the institutional and cultural levels, for example, are central to leadership choices. How teams go about balancing independent and interdependent behavior within the confines of these two contexts also helps members identify their leadership preferences and gauge the appropriateness of those preferences. Most important, leadership sets the team's personality by establishing its focus and the climate for the work.

Leader-led teams with a single team leader are the most easily understood and the most structured of these three models. While most organizations recognize the limitations of the dominant CEO who hands down directives to supervised implementation teams, that style is often transmitted throughout the organizational structure to managing supervisors who emulate—sometimes unconsciously—the commanding model. On these teams, the leader assumes responsibility for all decisions, strategies, and performance. Individual leaders are free to set management procedures and often leave their own style imprint on the team. Katzenbach and Smith, however, offer some insight: "In our experience, no small group at any level or in any part of an organization can fully succeed without learning to integrate and use both single-leader group discipline and team discipline as performance situations dictate."[5]

Consensus-led teams are by far the most flexible units because members begin with a shared understanding of mission, procedure, and authority. Teams determine which decisions or actions are appropriate for consensus and devise specific steps for achieving agreement. Consensus can help teams avoid problems with power differentials, status issues, and other process barriers. Teams with highly diverse members, however, typically take longer to form and to make decisions.

Managed teams use some of the elements of the other two models by applying a slightly different spin to task definition: Instead of members representing functional expertise (and therefore departmental authority) on cross-functional teams, for example, members represent team areas and interests. Rather than designing the marketing strategy for the team, then, a team member may become strategy manager or resource manager, giving her or him clear lines of independent responsibility while also maintaining interdependence on and with the other team members.

Individual members certainly have preconceptions, even if unstated, about leadership preferences based on previous experiences, projects, or assumptions. If teams administer a survey on team attitudes toward leadership or teamwork, the results provide an anonymous way of collecting views and marking patterns. Otherwise, members should at least discuss their opinions openly, without fear of judgment, correctness, or other retribution. The more autonomy given to team members, according to Harvard Professor Linda Hill, the more important it is they all commit to a common agenda. More effective teams, she notes, tend to be more flexible; they balance the authority between the manager and the team in ways best suited to the issue at hand.[6]

WHAT STRATEGIES WILL WE NEED FOR THIS EFFORT?

With teammates already firmly entrenched in the activities of forming, shaping, structuring, and adjusting team design, members need to draft informed and appropriate communication strategies for their work-based perceived skills and needs, strengths and challenges, documentation, and resources.

Developing effective team strategies, the heart of any team performance, requires clear communication among members and continual monitoring. If left undefined, teams often wind up later with misunderstandings about what process they've agreed to use or with reactive behavior, as opposed to responsive strategy. For the results to be clear, teams must identify these before setting evaluation procedures, since the procedures must be appropriate for measuring the team's results against strategic benchmarks. Planning team processes is a time-consuming but essential activity for helping members achieve three preliminary objectives: (1) establish a dynamic climate for accomplishing the work when together; (2) create clear task definitions and roles, and (3) provide the team with concrete evidence of members' initial progress.

WHAT EVALUATION PROCEDURES WILL WE USE TO MEASURE SUCCESS?

To maximize their opportunity for success, teams should set measures up front for evaluation and establish a system to measure and record how others will gauge their efforts. Using an institutional context is critical here: If a team expects a different performance management system than has been used previously on similar team efforts, then members must clearly explain the reasons for measuring this work differently, as well as raise appropriate questions for reframing appraisal issues.

- What set of procedures is necessary to support and appraise the teamwork?
- What policies might be affected by the outcomes?
- What kinds of data are needed to reflect the extrinsic benefits of the teamwork to the organization?
- What data is needed to measure the intrinsic benefits?
- How will the team collect, record, and maintain records?
- How long will this process take?
- What formats would most effectively present the team results and benefits?

To monitor and assess team performance challenges as well as behaviors, internal evaluation forms can help teams document progress. More important, such periodic checks provide written logs to reference for later recommendations, reporting activities, and outcome measurements. Members should communicate openly and frequently: If two members often spend time together discussing the project but do not share these points with the team, different perspectives may eventually emerge. New managers, in particular, may spend a great deal of time talking and connecting with a few selected members and base decisions or opinions primarily on these exchanges. This is particularly problematic if issues that are truly team concerns are never brought directly to the team: "Not surprisingly," says Professor Linda Hill, "many new managers frequently find themselves making decisions based on unnecessarily limited information and are often unpleasantly surprised to learn that actions directed at one subordinate have unintended negative impact on the morale or performance of their other subordinates."[7]

If the team is using internal and external assessment documents (see sample TeamComm tools at the end of this chapter), such records provide effective and familiar reminders of strategic progress and of the integral connection among team analysis (procedures and goal setting), implementation, and evaluation. Just as a team's reported outcomes grow directly from action plans conceived during the initial formation, the progress logs, if they are comprehensive, specific, and detailed, provide the foundation for the final report.

REFINING TEAMCOMM OPPORTUNITIES

TeamComm strategies articulate a team's priorities, its common language ("What do you mean by *crisis*?"), its responsiveness to competition, and its reactions to changes in resources or deadlines. The degree to which a team formalizes these practices, of course, should also be consistent with its institutional culture. But even with a broad outline of ideas in place, most groups still have several opportunities to refine the process of managing communication and transforming individuals into teams.

Typically, most new teams face six junctures critical to managing relationships, moments in a team's life cycle that will determine how the members work together and whether the team will fulfill its potential. We can classify these moments according to the kinds of behavior the team engages in: connecting, defining, communicating, conflicting, energizing, and evaluating. Reviewing these helps individual members redefine their attitudes toward the work process as a beginning (rather than a continuation of a previous experience), as well as to distance the formation phase from the work phase, to reenergize members, and to develop fresh perspectives to bring to the team. Each moment offers distinct opportunities that may evaporate later unless team members seize them. At the very least, they help establish the communication norm the team will use as it develops its work and tracks its performance.

Assuming that core skills are in place, teams can create gateways to good communication and achieve synergy more easily by focusing on the following areas when crafting appropriate and comprehensive team activities. Close attention to each opportunity helps to remind members of previous assumptions, to refresh memories, and, perhaps, to readjust earlier perceptions.

CONNECTING

LISTEN ACTIVELY

Everything begins here. No faking. It's possible, of course, to listen without hearing, just as it is possible to hear without listening. Actively doing both, however, involves various communication skills: linguistic awareness, nonverbal communication, and mental sharpness.

Team members can hone their skills through listening practice. They can participate in sessions to develop a higher awareness of point of view, clarity, recall, and summary. Through repetitive drills, teammates can train one another to listen attentively for different things: ideas, facts, specifics, innuendo, position, gaps, connections, competing interests, and problems. One such exercise involves working with a partner—each person speaks for ten minutes without interruption, then the listener repeats the major points spoken, including as many supporting details and facts as possible. While it isn't necessary to use the speaker's exact words, listeners learn very quickly to listen for content, to identify organization, and to remember evidentiary material. Over time, the drill also improves speakers' abilities to get to the point, to organize ideas, and to clearly indicate emphases.

If good managers spend most of their time listening and managers often spend much of their time working with and on teams, why, then, is it so difficult for team members to listen to one another? Why does it require practice in skill building?

Few people . . . have had much training in listening. Living in a competitive culture, most of us are most of the time chiefly concerned with getting our own view across, and we tend to find other people's speeches a tedious interruption of our own ideas.

    — S. I. Hayakawa[8] ▲

In addition to lacking listening training, we also fail to practice active listening because it requires additional time, focus, discernment, energy, self-discipline, and patience—commodities we are all in short supply of these days. To break the cycle of poor listening habits, then, team members need to do more than acknowledge that these skills are important: They need to do something about it. That may mean taking a listening assessment test. It also means building good habits into team activities and practices.

Develop a New Attitude

Perhaps the most important element for active listening is having the right attitude about it. Wanting to hear what others have to say is quite different from waiting for them to stop speaking. Being receptive to new ideas (or old ones heard before) helps open new pathways to thinking.

Read and Give Accurate Nonverbal Signs

Depending on which studies you read, we take in as much as 90% of our information through nonverbal communication. As we continue to rely more and more on visual and aural synthesizing, we send and receive messages in sound bites, expressions, and visual cues more often than we realize. This is true for teams as well. If we are operating under time constraints, we are likely to be less patient in listening to one another; less interested in anything that doesn't seem to bring closure in less than a few seconds; and less aware that our faces, gestures, and body language may speak louder and more eloquently than our voices.

Team members must be especially careful in early meetings to make and to send accurate nonverbal signals, since gestures, body language, and facial expressions convey powerful messages before teams begin to talk. But nonverbal interaction also serves another function: If we are *physically* involved in reacting and responding to others, we also have a stronger mental connection to what they say. In other words, we actually take in more information.

Check Egos Before Entering

Members more intent on expressing their own viewpoints than on hearing others' make poor listeners. To be receptive to other thinking means being released from vested interests—including how others perceive us. If the ego is not preoccupied with making an impression, listening skills improve, as well as performance results. (Team members should bear in mind that some egos, despite their large size, are fragile and may require special handling.) Still, our natural instinct is to contribute our ideas first and then listen. At its most acute, active listening allows one to understand another point of view by inhabiting the same mental space as the speaker—in short, to understand that there is more than one reality.

DEFINING

Set, Observe, and Enforce Ground Rules

If a team understands its charter or mission, agreements at the outset about process and behavior help prevent confusion later and pave the way for a smooth transition to problem solving. If members are reluctant to ask questions or to insist on clarity because of power or status differences, the team may pay a heavy price when it's too late to correct ill-conceived beginnings. Specific ground rules are also essential in order to establish trust among members and to avoid certain kinds of miscommunication.

A good ground rule is "What is said here stays here."

Members comfortable enough to share personal information with team members may not appreciate hearing that same information repeated outside the team setting. Similarly, if a product idea is in development, teams may not want others from different departments tinkering with it or judging it before it's ready.

There's no crying in baseball!
— Jimmy Dugan (Tom Hanks),
A League of Their Own ▲

In order to establish procedures, team members need to set a plan for basic activities: how they will make decisions, how they will proceed, when they will meet, how they will communicate conflict, how they will meet their goals, how they will measure progress. Some teams appoint a facilitator or a parliamentarian to monitor team observances of protocol and ground rules. If the team gets off track, the facilitator is the recognized messenger to correct the course.

ESTABLISH TEAM VALUES AND PROCEDURES

To eliminate some of the misunderstandings when setting priorities and procedures, teams can also determine how closely they agree on major team activities without relying on guesswork. This also helps establish a means of depersonalizing issues that may arise later from those presenting them; in short, separating problems from the people. After all, it is far better to say, "I can't support that solution," than it is to say, "I can't support you."[9] More important, using an objective methodology for determining team values frees all individuals from potential accusations of aggression or dominance.

By using a simple form to establish the order and the assigned value of each team activity, members then compare rankings. (See **Assessment Form #6**: Establishing Team Values.) Through discussion and consensus, or in some cases, mathematical averaging of ranked scores, teams agree from the beginning on the procedures they will use to get the work done. Implicitly, this sets up a problem-solving sequence. Some organizations using this method to determine what's important to the team also compare management's ranking of the activities on the list with the team's responses.

DESIGNATE ROLES

If teams have already answered the leadership question, designating individual roles or task assignments follows as a natural extension of leadership structure. A single leader, for example, might appoint task areas or ask for volunteers. Consensus-led teams use a process in keeping with their decision-making procedures, whereas self-managed teams might align their functional responsibilities with project parameters. All three, however, would design structural roles in accordance with assessment results, project goals or team charter, and company or organizational structure. (For a model of complementary team positions, see **Assessment Form #7**: TeamComm Partnerships.)

The most successful teams, of course, are able to maintain a careful balance between authority and discretion and don't confuse leadership with functional expertise. Some decisions are best made through consensus, while others are reached through consultation with the members most affected. As Professor Hill points out, some managers get input from the team members

ASSESSMENT FORM #6
Establishing Team Values

What is important to you?
Order each activity on the following chart sequentially from 1 to 20.

Activity	Individual View	Team View
Establish decision-making policies.		
Assess strengths and weaknesses.		
Set timelines.		
Identify team needs.		
Make contingency plans.		
Measure outcomes.		
Study external conditions.		
Plan strategies.		
Facilitate problem solving.		
Set reporting procedures.		
Develop conflict rules.		
Define project goals.		
Set meeting agendas.		
Determine resources.		
Identify team members.		
Organize collaborative sessions.		
Identify leadership.		
Recommend action.		
Assign task responsibility and accountability.		
Other (Specify)		

ASSESSMENT FORM #7
TeamComm Partnerships

Phase I: Forming Roles and Responsibilities

After administering the assessment tools and individual profiles, teams can increase their efficiency in setting procedures by forming partnerships based on specific team positions. To ensure balanced team perspectives, work experiences and cultural backgrounds, and skill sets, each team should base position assignments partly on the data from the assessment tools.

Each team determines its own TeamComm strategies (decision making, meeting procedures, conflict management, etc.). While not all positions suggested may be necessary or useful to small teams, each should designate a communications manager, a team manager, and any other functional positions the team designates. Some teams may wish to combine positions or duties or to establish different configurations based on their skill sets and needs.

Communications Managers (CoMs)

Responsibilities include collecting accurate and appropriate communication information (channel choices, accessibility, schedules, etc.) for the team and for organizational distribution. Each representative is responsible for maintaining up-to-date information on team members, including changes in addresses, status, or affiliation. Information shared from the various assessment tools is at participants' discretion.

Team Managers (TMs)

Responsibilities include negotiating with the other members and managers for team preferences on procedures; decision-making; external negotiations; assuring team understanding and compliance with procedures, tasks, and assignments; and representing the team's position during debriefings and discussions. Team managers clarify mission, methods, and practices.

Document and Feedback Managers (DMs)

Responsibilites include ensuring that each member of the team has copies of tools, appropriate documents, papers, handouts, and other resources provided by the members of the team. This member also uses a variety of media to record team meetings, including videotaping, audiotaping, or other means.

Web Managers (WMs)

Serve as a web resource contact for team members by searching, collecting, storing, or posting resource information. Maintain any web communications (bulletin boards, chat rooms, linked sites) needed by the team and coordinate such activities among members.

Climate Managers (CLMs)

Help the team maintain an optimum learning climate by encouraging team communication, energizing members, building group cohesiveness, ensuring cultural awareness of differences in proxemics, nonverbal communication, customs, as well as monitoring energy and attentiveness. (This could also involve literal climate: ensuring physical comfort zones by monitoring the thermostat.)

Conflict Managers (CMs)

Ensure that each team has a procedure or mechanism for resolving conflicts. These managers serve as mediators, dispute resolution officers, or negotiators, depending on the nature of the conflict. Managers may also wish to meet with other team conflict managers to establish some class standards or ground rules.

Phase II: Managing TeamComm Procedures

With positions and responsibilities in place, teams can proceed with setting operational procedures. Team leaders may choose to negotiate separately among team members in order to present a consensus position to the team.

Phase III: Performing

All members take responsibility for completion of tasks, training, updates, meetings, and reporting. Team managers report results or appoint a member to do so.

Phase IV: Reporting and Evaluating

Teams set individual or group specifications for formal and informal reporting requirements, including format, length, design, and production. In addition to the organization's requirements, teams need to spend time evaluating their efforts as a team. All tasks for the project are managed by the team and through its decision-making procedures.

These four phases should ensure optimal conditions for effective team communication during the process.

and discuss different alternatives with them but retain the role of ultimate decision maker, while others make decisions without consulting team members.

BE ALERT TO SIGNS OF GROUPTHINK

While groupthink[10]—that seductive, unreflective, uncritical behavior that can create paralysis for teams—is more likely to occur in homogeneous groups, it can also be a side effect of over-regulating interaction. If members become too supportive of one another, for example, they stop confronting each other. In very cohesive groups, according to experts, when strong norms to preserve harmonious relationships evolve, members may start to suppress critical thinking or critical expression.[11]

Attitudes toward conflict provide another instructive example. If members who equate lack of confrontation or conflict with team success establish the team climate, they can derail any team—ethnocentric or cross-cultural—by shutting down constructive dialogue and TeamComm potential before it begins. Some team members find it less disruptive to provide a specific place or time on the agenda for uninhibited free exchange and problem identification.

COMMUNICATING

AVOID EITHER/OR COMMUNICATION

Few people who dominate discussions or decisions see themselves as inflexible or unreasonable. In the attempt to lead or to get the group unstuck, these strong personalities are usually motivated, enthusiastic, and well-meaning. If the team does not validate choosing one idea over another because it's the only way (perhaps it is the only way that's been discussed), these types are easier to manage. If a team does not set up processes that force mutually exclusive choices, it doesn't practice bad analytical habits.

> **Team Quote ▼**
>
> *There is hardly a person who does not think more of what he wants to say than of his answer to what is said.*
> — LaRochefoucault[12] ▲

SEEK INCLUSION AS A BEST PRACTICE

Members need to respect differences in perspective, expression, style, and experiences. Unless members look at all sides of an issue and have access to each member's thinking, simply avoiding either/or decisions or avoiding disagreements will not ensure participation or understanding. Including different perspectives enhances creativity, stretches self-imposed boundaries, and reveals underlying views that may otherwise go unspoken.

Research on how diversity affects teams has largely focused on task definition, functional performance, and group dynamics—particularly when dealing with transnational teams. Transnational teams consist of employees working for the same company but in different countries. We still have much to study here. However, since effective TeamComm embraces cultural differences as a team precept, the higher the awareness, the greater the potential for genuine synergy. Again, the kind of team is also important when managing transnational or cross-cultural teams. Consensus teams may face the greatest process challenges in these cases, but they also stand to gain the greatest learning opportunities since the team must actively consider all perspectives in its decisions.[13]

Insofar as nationalities inform each individual's perceptions, values, norms, behavior, and assumptions, transnational teams can raise members' performance through a broader understanding of the skill sets involved. In many cases, teams with a marginal familiarity or limited appreciation of these differences produce mediocre or suboptimal performances; such teams either fail to recognize the benefits and challenges presented by multiple nationalities, assign collective cultural attributes to individual team members, or identify the effort as too time-consuming before it starts.

USE A COMMON LANGUAGE

A common language will develop among members of a team whether or not they recognize it, label it, or consciously use it. Some teams include this as part of the process of setting ground rules, while others never consider it a formal characteristic of their communication.

The industry or culture naturally provides the basic rubric, but a common language is more than industry jargon. If developed over time, common language can provide a shorthand way of referencing complex or high-context discussions for teams who speak it. Team culture can enrich and expand its vocabulary through code words and metaphors as a way of protecting new products, referencing experimental designs, equating current market climate to historical conditions, or creating stronger relationships.

Technology teams at Microsoft are probably most widely known for Microspeak as its buzzwords leak out, find use in translation, and stick. Two examples may be helpful here; both were developed in 2000: *facemail* (speaking face to face) and *fiber media* (paper documents). These terms illustrate both a referent and an attitude shared by those who understand and use them.

A common language, then, can also create fun for teams who enjoy their work and enjoy talking about it. But dangers lurk in overuse or inappropriate settings. Precisely because it is a language shared by a few, outsiders can misunderstand messages as designed to exclude them or even to refer to them. If the language interferes with or clouds communication with others—even if not intended for them—it can make a team appear frivolous. While the Internetgentsia, those well-versed in dot.com semantics, produce new meanings at zip speed, common sense can contribute much to common language.

SEEK AND PROVIDE MEANINGFUL FEEDBACK

When listening, discussing, or presenting information, teams must interact to be fully integrated. This means not merely sitting together but also thinking *with* and *for* one another. Teams can accomplish this through many practices, but here are a few of the best:

- By repeating key phrases or words, both speakers and listeners can give guidance to one another and signal areas of emphasis.
- By withholding judgment or avoiding a critical tone while not ignoring gaps in logic, evidence, or conclusions, team members can also train one another to prepare for work sessions, meetings, and next steps.
- Reframing issues or statements that may not be clear or may have been misunderstood also helps ensure that everyone heard the same thing and in the same context.
- Finally, learning one another's habitual patterns—whether in speaking or in listening—also guides the team to function more effectively as a working unit. Offering gentle reminders that someone is off track, off task, or just generally digressing helps everyone refocus.

USE E-COMMUNICATION TO DEVELOP TEAM COMMUNICATION

Global business is already a redundant phrase. If business is global, teams must communicate globally, domestically, and locally. With traditional borders largely collapsed through cyber connections and e-commerce, new economy strategies and perspectives have also increased the number and kinds of communication demands teams must embrace.

Communication contexts should now be less ethnocentric, but old habits die hard, and teams should be particularly alert to multicultural differences in context. Global and niched players must be constantly alert to international changes, treaties, shifting economies, political pressures, privacy issues, and security issues. Furthermore, teams need to be aware of the impact of technological developments on their core competencies, technical positioning, interpersonal skills, interpretations, and decision making. Just as important, members should work to understand and respect basic differences in attitudes that affect life and work styles, for example, attitudes toward time (temporal orientation), space (proxemics), language (level of familiarity), and technology. Such differences, we should remember, are national, cultural, and regional, but also individual.

And as the new economy redefines our understanding of pace in business processes, it also drives corresponding change in business communication processes and practices. Software that coordinates teamwork through shareware, bulletin boards, discussion boards, internal or external distribution lists, and group decision consensus tools can create fewer cracks in a team's foundation, but joint discussions take more time to read and may be inefficient or inappropriate for many teams who need to communicate individually or face to face. Some teams seem to prefer the advantage of synchronous communication as a supplement to—not a substitute for—interpersonal contact. Transnational teams, employees working in different countries, are key sources of communication performance strategies, and the new transnational paradigm—virtual teams communicating across traditionally defined boundaries without cultural or geographic anxieties—will yield increasingly innovative refinements in TeamComm strategies.

CONFLICTING

EMPTY THE TRASH—DON'T BURY IT

When an interpersonal issue comes up, it's usually better to deal with it up front, calmly, by following the team's ground rules. If left to decay, garbage not only smells, it leaves a lingering stench. But if teams handle early challenges effectively, they can move on confidently and without anxiety to the next issue. Perception is as important as intent in injury, and if team members trust one another, they can communicate this.

In so doing, teammates must also practice clear, nonconfrontational communication. Raising a point that is potentially explosive shouldn't invite defensiveness by launching a personal attack. Team members should identify appropriate ways of raising these issues—using appropriate language—when they establish ground rules.

> **Team Quote** ▼
>
> *I've always been too confrontational, especially when I know I'm right.*
>
> — Bob Knight, former Indiana University basketball coach[14] ▲

ANTICIPATE CONTINGENCIES

TeamComm strategies directly correlate to available resources. If shortages begin to occur or inventory suddenly dwindles, competitive attitudes among teams within the organization, as well as among members of the same team, may emerge. Even though teams know conflict is likely to emerge over such shortages, they may be unprepared for the changes in attitude, trust, comfort, and, possibly, procedure.

If members must adjust their direction suddenly, they should do so collectively with full disclosure. Team cohesion fragments easily if group processes are ignored or unconsciously by-passed. A fuller discussion of team issues and conflict follows in Chapter 3.

ENERGIZING

AP-*PRAISE* THE WORK WHILE WORKING

Regardless of the effort to keep the big picture in full focus, people naturally develop competitive myopia on teams. Remember that the effort will outlive the team—the ultimate goal is not simply this team's success. The praise should be specific and genuine, however, rather than hollow. Recognizing good work is quite different from vague or overstated encouragement that can make team members feel singled out without justification.

CELEBRATE MILESTONES

Sustaining the effort is different from managing the team's processes. Over time, teams can lose their edge for many reasons. Astute managers, leaders, and members must recognize the need to mark the team's progress as well as its challenges. Even if these milestones are simply mini-goals or timeline updates, unexpected recognition and individual or group commendations for work in progress energize the ongoing work, even if temporarily. Make sure the celebrations are authentic: Praising one another's efforts habitually, without reason, undermines the group's trust and respect.

EVALUATING

PRACTICE, PRACTICE, PRACTICE

Even if teams aren't headed for Carnegie Hall, the advice is still valid. Similarly, just as sports teams must work out regularly to turn in a good performance, members must flex communication muscles habitually and consciously. While practice may not make perfect, it makes for steady progress. Regular sessions or exercises to improve weak skills benefit the individual and the team. If left to atrophy, these muscles suffer the same fate as tissue. The lesson from strength training applies here as well: Use it or lose it. Good team communication skills, like good teams, don't simply evolve or magically coalesce. They require hard work and careful attention.

DETERMINE YOUR TEAM'S OWN OUTCOMES

A team intent on destroying the competition pays a heavy price: Losing the potential for collaboration and innovation diminishes current efforts as well as future enterprises. The us versus them at-all-costs mentality contributes neither to the overall well-being of the team nor to its achievements. Teams in the twenty-first century will reach full potential in the marketplace through alliances, partnerships, mutual improvements, and shared resources. (For tracking performance, see **Assessment Form #8**: Measuring Internal Effectiveness and **Assessment Form #9**: Measuring External Effectiveness.)

ASSESSMENT FORM #8
Measuring Internal Effectiveness

Rank the following on a scale of 1 to 5 for assessments real or perceived.

Scale: Evidence supports that we . . .
5 – are effective in our demonstrated abilities.
4 – are relatively effective in our abilities.
3 – are somewhat effective in our abilities.
2 – are potentially ineffective unless we make improvements.
1 – are ineffective.

Internal Assessment	1	2	3	4	5
Performance Appraisals					
Peer Appraisals					
Department Reports					
Trainers					
Shareholders					

ASSESSMENT FORM #9
Measuring External Effectiveness

Rank the following on a scale of 1 to 5 for assessments real or perceived.

Scale: Evidence supports that we . . .
5 – are effective in our demonstrated abilities.
4 – are relatively effective in our abilities.
3 – are somewhat effective in our abilities.
2 – are potentially ineffective unless we make improvements.
1 – are ineffective.

External Assessment	1	2	3	4	5
Client/Customer Appraisals					
Partners/Alliances					
Team/Industry Benchmarks					
Media Coverage					
Independent Assessors (Consultants)					

Microsoft: An Extreme Case or a Lesson Learned?

How did one of the world's most successful teams wind up at the center of the century's most violent anti-trust storm? If we place Microsoft's primary communication problem—the disconnection between public perception and self-image—the company's breakdown occurs squarely between the model's institutional and cultural levels.

Microsoft sees itself as providing value and promoting innovation by protecting its products and services. The legal view, delivered in stunningly clear language by Judge Thomas Penfield Jackson, is that Microsoft squelched its competitors through corrupt business practices and tactics (by illegally tying Explorer to Windows, giving advance Windows data updates to developers, and harming competitors by improperly using an exclusive contract with computer makers). The company's enemies are now legion and very vocal, including Oracle's Larry Ellison and Netscape's Forester Schadler, who see Microsoft's unrepentant attitude continuing. In Schadler's view, Microsoft's .Net initiative is simply the latest indication of an isolated, self-enclosed perspective: "The executive team is having trouble adopting the values of the Internet."[15]

How the Microsoft case will affect future strategies and alliances in the technology industry will evolve for years to come. But the lesson is instructive for those who disdain potential collaborative communication within their industry: Microsoft's failure to navigate the sometimes turbulent and unpredictable waters of competitive communication within its own culture has left it with powerful enemies, reluctant allies, and a wary consumer base.

Note: The company's code names for new technologies are just one example of its attitude: Office 2000's new application for installing/uninstalling software is Darwin. Survival not merely of the fittest, but of those best able to adapt to changing environments may be more than an attitude here. It may also be a strategy. ▲

Some teams find creating their own detailed, written guidelines for routine activities helpful to their own performance expectations, such as the following:

- Meeting procedures
- Accountability and nondisclosure agreements
- Problem-solving/conflict models
- Progress reporting methods
- Progress logs for action plans (See **Assessment Form #10.**)
- E-mail protocol, including team rules and procedures (See, for example, **Assessment Form #11:** Priscilla Rogers' E-mail Guidelines for International Project Teams.)

ASSESSMENT FORM #10
Progress Log for Action Plans

Record team activities directly related to the project.

Scale:
5 – I am completely confident in my ability.
4 – I am confident in my ability.
3 – I am somewhat confident in my ability.
2 – I am confident that I could improve my ability.
1 – I am not confident in my ability.

Skill	**Activity or Event**	Include examples or a specific context where appropriate.
Written Work:		
E-mail		
Reports		
Other		
Oral Communication:		
Interpersonal		
Presentations		
Other		
Change Communication (policies, procedures, etc.)		
Collaboration		
Conflict Management		
Diversity Issues		
Technology Use:		
Web Usage		
Groupware		
Databases		
Consensus Software		
Other		
Listening Skills		
Media Relations		
Negotiations		
Nonverbal Skills		
Performance Evaluations/Feedback		
Team Issues		

ASSESSMENT FORM #11
E-mail Guidelines for International Project Teams*

For international project teams, e-mail comprises one of the most critical methods of communicating, particularly between project teams and their supervisors. A casual or cavalier attitude toward e-mail can lead to unprofessional usage, which will significantly impact supervisory evaluations and the ultimate success of a project.

Analysis of IMAP (International Multidisciplinary Action Projects) e-mail communications show that participants could greatly benefit by reviewing the following information regarding efficient, clear, appropriate, and professional e-mail use.

E-MAIL CONTENT

"Talk" with "Subject:"
- Use the subject line to say as much as possible about the message (e.g., rather than "scope statement" use a "talking" version such as "scope stmt/1st draft" or "revised scope statement").
- If reader action is required, use a verb—e.g., "*comment* on attached" or "*need* input re slides".
- Only use an old subject line or reference line (say to reply to someone's message) if it is highly relevant. Usually a revised subject line is required for effective communication.

Use first line to introduce
- Use the first line or two to state what the message is about.
- If the topic is new, you have to introduce it.
- If the topic is old, you have to tell the reader what earlier message(s) it regards.
- Don't begin with "Yes, that's fine," or "I agree." or "Let's go ahead with it." The reader may have no idea what "it" means.
- Readers need an introduction immediately after the subject line unless you want them to waste time trying to figure out "what the heck you're talking about."

Write top down
- Write "top down" (high-impact style), putting your most important information first.
- Try to get everything significant on the first screen. Some e-mail readers don't scroll down. Many e-mail readers slack off after several screens. Many e-mail readers forget what you said first or get distracted.

Write in short chunks
- Write in short chunks using short lines, short sentences, and short paragraphs. If your message is long or complicated, use lists, numbering, and headings.
- Every new start is likely to catch reader attention. Content in the middle of paragraphs is buried and may be overlooked.

* Priscilla S. Rogers, University of Michigan Business School. Developed to assist International Project Teams discuss their communication effectiveness, these e-mail guidelines drew heavily on teaching notes for e-mail use written by Jone Rymer for the management communication course at Wayne State University.

Forecast/number content

- If you have several important points or questions, forecast and number them.
- *Forecast:* "We've made the following 6 discoveries this week. . . ."
- *Number:* "(1) The need to investigate the XYZ is less important to ABC . . . (2) Finding out about TTT is critical for the project, however. This is a surprise. . . ."
- *Forecast:* "We have 3 questions. . . . "
- *Number:* "(1) What do you mean by "turn your headings into claims? (2) Should our abstract include our key findings?"

Avoid all CAPS

- All CAPS are just plain difficult to read.
- Keyboard your message in standard caps and lowercase letters.

Limit "embedding"

- Limit the practice of integrating a response into a message from someone else.
- Embedding may be efficient for you—you don't have to rekey some lines.
- Embedding is not efficient for the reader who must search for your reply.
- Highlighting embedded text doesn't ensure that it will be highlighted by the technology the reader is using.
- To save rekeying, use cut and paste rather than embedding.

"Sign" it

- Ending your message with your individual or team name may seem needless, but it isn't, especially if your e-mail name is not identical with the name you're called.

E-MAIL MANAGEMENT

Check e-mail at least once a day

- E-mail is your lifeline, especially during international projects.
- If your supervisors e-mail you and you don't reply, you're still communicating. No communication is communication—e.g., Supervisor: "That ABC team must be goofing off."

Use a feedback loop

- Acknowledge when e-mail is received even if you can't respond immediately—e.g., "Will reply Monday."
- If a response is not required or explicitly requested, some kind of acknowledgment may still be wise—e.g., "Got it. Thx."

Wait, resend if no reply

- If you don't get a reply to an important e-mail, wait. After a reasonable period, resend the message. If silence continues, resend with a note that you haven't received a reply.
- In an emergency, make a phone call or fax.
- Remember, one of e-mail's advantages is the reader need not respond immediately. Your reader may not be ready to answer you.

Get permission to quote/forward some e-mail

- Don't automatically quote or forward others' e-mails without permission, *unless it is obvious that such sharing is expected by the sender*—e.g., If you're the communications manager for the team, you'd obviously forward directions regarding your deliverables to your other team members.

E-MAIL TONE

Check level of formality

- Consider what level of formality your reader expects. Write accordingly.
- Much e-mail is conversational including: personal pronouns ("I," "you," "we"); contractions ("We're" rather than "We are"); parenthetical asides ("We concluded that we should . . . —as you probably expected."); and active rather than passive constructions (Active: "We moved the background section to the end." Passive: "The background section was moved to the end.").
- Other e-mail is for formal purposes; style should reflect this (e.g., work groups use e-mail ballots; consultants use e-mail to contact clients; field teams use e-mail to confirm/ document deadlines for deliverables).

Converse, don't chat

- Joking and casual language may not carry over well into e-mail.
- In face-to-face conversation, work groups can get quite informal. When work groups transition to e-mail, however, the jokes and language are *documented, free of nonverbal cues,* and *can be distributed.*
- Employees have been fired for unprofessional/offensive e-mails. The New York Times Co. fired 22 employees at their Norfolk office, plus one in New York. Roughly 20 more employees, who the company determined had received offensive messages and did nothing, got warning letters (*WSJ,* "Prying Times" 02/04/2000)
- Write e-mails more like you write paper memos, rather than like you may chat at the pub. E-mail may be a conversational style, but it is never face-to-face conversation.

Compensate for lack of tone

- Compensate for the lack of vocal tone and nonverbal cues by selecting words carefully. E-mail includes no gestures, facial expressions, and tone of voice to help interpret your meaning. There is no immediate give and take as in face-to-face conversation.
- *Emoticons* (:) = smile) may help, but they can also hinder. Too many emoticons can reduce the professional quality of an e-mail. Emoticons can be interpreted as a bit too cute, thus hurting writer credibility.
- *Flaming* (minor misunderstandings that turn into online confrontations) results because e-mail writers didn't consider how their words may be interpreted (or misinterpreted).

CREATING AND MEASURING PERFORMANCE

Team success depends on the validity of the operational processes and the performance measures the team recognizes, understands, and respects. Eventually, the buck stops and the team must understand how it got there.

Team Quote ▼

People have a need to work in teams. There is a desire to work with others and enjoy the benefits of your work and your successes together with people who enjoy the same benefits. These satisfactions are as important today as they have ever been and I believe they will stay important.
— Andrew Grove, Chairman and cofounder of Intel Inc.[16] ▲

Although measuring performance can be the least pleasant part of the team process—and the step most often shortchanged—it needn't be. In fact, it should be the most beneficial part of the process if it produces learning, validates the effort, and creates a sense of well-being. Most would agree, however, that both managers and members are more effective if they observe some mutual precepts to measure their efforts.

Members need opportunities to revisit performance results as individuals and as a unit. Otherwise, they may be left with a sense of incompletion, genuine confusion, or misconceptions about the success or failure of the team or organizational assessment. Even more important, teams need to access performance indicators during the process rather than wait until the process is over to gauge the results. Simply put, "teams that engage in self-monitoring and self-correcting of their process and performance are more effective than those that do not."[17]

Again, some teams prefer using formal mechanisms for this process; others, more informal methods. Some teams chart their progress—and their self-assessments—formally during the work stages. Depending on a team's culture, its size, and its preferences, assessment tools can also provide a way for the team to conduct its work or to refocus its strategies if major changes occur in the external or internal environment. Other teams prefer to use such tools as a formal closure to the group's work, or to assess different phases of a project, if the work is ongoing.

ESTABLISH AN APPROPRIATE SYSTEM TO MEASURE SUCCESS

Members of a project team may be convinced they have created the best possible campaign with an innovative marketing strategy for a new product, but if consumers don't recognize the product or buy it, the results will be clear. That doesn't necessarily mean the team failed. It may mean that the team failed to meet one set of performance goals, that it recognized a different set of priorities for this project, or that it ignored a fundamental system of external appraisal.

In a study of four different kinds of work teams, Cohen and Bailey found that teams with healthy internal processes rate their own performance high, and while objective measures are appropriate tools for measuring quantitative goals, sometimes "perceptions of effectiveness from key stakeholders" are more important.[18] Clearly, what most teams need is an appropriate method for measuring their effectiveness both internally and externally.

USE THE RIGHT STRATEGIC TOOLS

The TeamComm model places a team's efforts within a context of performance. If a team loses sight of its external constituents, then it may need to pinpoint when that happened and how. If, however, this was an experiment to test the team's ability to balance multiple perspectives, to restart concept creativity, to build teams eager to work together again, or to measure the validity of focus group data, the team may legitimately be called effective *and* successful.

SHARE PERFORMANCE RESULTS AS WELL AS THE MISSION

While perceptions may vary as to the outcomes, on trivial as well as nontrivial details, members should take care to clarify their positions. If members disagree as to the overall success of a project, or of the effort, chances are they buried earlier departures from the mission or the process. As team processes evolve and the team settles into its norms, members exercise options and explore interpretations in keeping with their own communication styles and preferences. Periodic comparisons of data, research, methods, and analyses are key to ensuring a team's authenticity, as well as its accuracy in self-assessment.

If a team uses a formal self-monitoring tool, for example, data gathered through this process should be shared orally as a group. Any clarifications and adjustments would help reassure some members and validate others. Also, if the individual graphs all intersect at the same point—say, external analysis—then the team needs to focus its energies on translating its mission more clearly to key stakeholders.

Finally, remember that individuals, regardless of team membership, measure satisfaction with an outcome based on the standards we use to judge it. If one individual focuses on gains, while another focuses on losses or unrealized expectations, reactions will vary substantially. Make sure all team members review the results *together* and agree on the interpretation as well as the details. Though sometimes difficult to do, members should try to regard mistakes or disappointments as learning opportunities, rather than excuses for failure or reasons for punishment.

DISCUSSION QUESTIONS

1. Visit a company's web pages and locate the elements of a communication strategy or protocol for that company. What features can you identify? Interview someone (either in person or electronically) who works at this company about how he or she uses teams. Compare the tools for team communication with those your colleagues find. What are the strengths and weaknesses of each?

2. Work with your team to develop an action plan for improving internal communication within an organization on campus or in your community. What sorts of information do you need before you begin?

3. Research a company's press releases for recent announcements introducing a new team. What kind of team is it? Is the team's mission clear? Who are the members? Is it clear from the announcement why they were chosen? Where does this team fit with the company's overall strategy?

ENDNOTES

1. Jim Kerstetter, with Peter Burrows, "HP's E-Speak: Good Products, Botched Marketing," *BusinessWeek,* July 3, 2000, 144.
2. J. R. Katzenbach and D. K. Smith, *The Wisdom of Teams: Creating the High-Performance Organization* (New York: HarperCollins, 1993, rpt. 1999), xvii.
3. James S. O'Rourke, *Management Communication: A Case Analysis Approach* (Upper Saddle River, NJ: Prentice-Hall, 2001), 1995.
4. Regina Maruca, *http://pf.fastcompany.com/online/40/one.html.*
5. Katzenbach and Smith, xxiv. "Too many managers . . . behave as though the selection of a team leader is the only thing that matters." (p. xvii).
6. Linda A. Hill, *Building Effective One-on-One Work Relationships,* Harvard Business School reprint, 9-497-028, October 13, 1996, 3.
7. Linda A. Hill, *Managing Your Team,* Harvard Business School Teaching Note 9-494-081, rev. March 28, 1995, 2.
8. S. I. Hayakawa, "How to Attend a Conference," *http://www.listen.org/pages/quotes.html.*
9. D. A. Whetten and K. S. Cameron, *Developing Management Skills: Managing Conflict* (New York: HarperCollins, 1993), 35.
10. I. L. Janis, *Victims of Groupthink* (Boston: Houghton Mifflin, 1972).
11. Ibid. For additional discussions on this issue, see also Adler; Hackman; Jehn and Mannix; Hill; Susan G. Cohen and Diane E. Bailey, "What Makes Teams Work: Group Effectiveness Research from the Shop Floor to the Executive Suite," *Journal of Management* 3, no.3 (1997): 239–290.
12. As quoted in Gerard I. Nierenberg, *The Art of Negotiating* (New York: Barnes and Noble, 1968), 47.
13. Opinions on the effectiveness of consensus management vary. As noted here, leadership decisions depend on the variables involved at all five levels of the systems model in Chapter 1. For differing views on consensus, see, for example, Linda Hill, "Managing Your Team," 11; and David A. Nadler's "High Performance Executive Teams," in *Corporate Board* (July–August 1992), and "The World of the CEO," with J. D. Heilpern, in D. A. Nadler, J. L. Spencer, and Associates (eds.), *Executive Teams* (San Francisco: Jossey-Bass, 1998).
14. Bob Knight, quoted in AP wire services after his dismissal as head basketball coach at Indiana University.
15. *BusinessWeek,* July 3, 2000, 144.
16. *BusinessWeek,* August 28, 2000, 214.
17. Hill, *Managing Your Team,* 9.
18. Cohen and Bailey, 282.

STRATEGIES FOR MANAGING TEAM CONFLICT

Approaches to managing conflict may seem at first to be as numerous as the kinds of conflict that occur in the workplace. Whether using the latest self-help workbook, theoretical systems models, or conflict paradigms specific to industry, teams need to understand, appreciate, and confront the unique position conflict occupies in any group effort. Assessing conflict styles, classifying competencies, and describing conflict strategies can help teams develop trust, improve performance, and decrease the likelihood that negative experiences will interrupt them.

Team Quote ▼

The secret of being a good manager is to keep the five guys who hate you away from the four who are undecided.
— Casey Stengel, former manager,
New York Yankees[1] ▲

Why is it essential for teams to include conflict management as an important part of their strategic planning? Unproductive conflict usually brings high costs—financial, psychological, social, sometimes medical, and even legal. The financial costs of organizational conflict can include wasted salary and benefits, wasted time and energy, loss of skilled employees, lost work time, lowered job motivation and performance, health costs, absenteeism, and theft or damage. According to the Dana Mediation Institute, in an example provided by a healthcare facility in New England, an incident between a doctor and two nurses cost $60,916.77 alone in terms of wasted workweek hours and loss of skilled employees.

Although we all have an intuitive understanding of conflict, even within cohesive teams, the members often surprise one another with their different attitudes toward conflict and toward those they perceive as conflict creators. Because of such differences, it is helpful to work from a specific premise: Team conflict arises when members become aware of discrepancies, incompatible wishes, or irreconcilable desires.[2] The TeamComm approach can diminish conflict episodes that derail, delay, or disintegrate groups and teams without diminishing creative kinds of conflict that can introduce contrary opinions or interpretations of data, or spur members toward better results. Groups and teams, then, need to agree on a strategy for managing conflict based on a shared understanding of what conflict really is.

In this chapter, we will look at some ways to classify group conflict, to analyze individual conflict styles, and to identify strategies for encouraging healthy conflict practices while diminishing disruptive episodes. Finally, we will consider specific categories of serious team communication conflict and provide some guidelines for counteracting the effects of workplace challenges.

CLASSIFYING CONFLICT IN GROUPS AND TEAMS

Implementing strategies may be easier for teams and groups if they initially identify conflict affecting team communication as one of two types: interpersonal or contextual. For most of us, the term *conflict* conjures images or episodes occurring between and because of two or more individuals; but conflict also arises from the environment in which teams work, the written forms of communication they use, and the system of operations through which they accomplish their work. These two types of conflict offer distinctly different challenges to teams experiencing differences of opinion, disagreements, misinterpretations, and competing interests. For teams to achieve breakthrough results, they must understand that the nature of the episode determines the management communication strategy.

> **Thinking About Teams** ▼
>
> *Hasso Plattner, SAP's co-CEO, provides an instructive example of a style that combines conflict with consensus: "While Plattner believes in obtaining consensus among his lieutenants, he doesn't care how much he irritates people along the way. In fact, his confrontational style is deliberate. 'He creates stressful situations. He fuels the discussions with provocative statements. Sometimes he's rigid, even rude. But it's about getting people engaged so they can be creative,' says Wolfgang Kemna, CEO of SAP America, a 13-year SAP veteran."*[7] ▲

- Interpersonal conflict occurs between or among members because of how their teammates perceive them: their personal traits, characteristics, and expressions, perceived as extensions of *self*.
- Contextual conflict occurs between or among members as a result of how their teammates perceive what they have *done or produced:* their product designs, reports, contracts, letters, drafts, blueprints, or other actions perceived as being objective, or disingenuous, or perhaps even conspiratorial.

Recent research also classifies team conflict according to patterns of behavior that emerge over time. Drawing on previous studies, Jehn and Mannix[3] tracked conflict episodes emerging in student teams at three U.S. business schools during one semester: "Teams performing were characterized by low but increasing levels of process conflict, low levels of relationship conflict, with a rise near project deadlines, and moderate levels of task conflict at the midpoint of group interaction."[4] These categories—relationship, task, and process—are relevant to workplace teams, as well, and especially useful to teams unable to separate the issues from the members or to supervisors uncertain about the sources of a team's difficulties.

Relationship conflict, of course, is the kind that first springs to mind. Personality clashes, previous experiences, and other emotional bases for tension or irritation are the usual culprits, and, while not necessarily rational, these can produce very real obstacles for effective team communication. Task conflict, as the name implies, identifies differences of opinion about the group's task[5] but usually excludes the volatile, emotional flare-ups associated with interpersonal conflict. Process conflicts arise from "an awareness of controversies about aspects of how task accomplishment will proceed."[6] The Team-Comm procedures and protocol discussed in the previous chapters can accommodate all three of these categories of conflict.

Team Quote ▼

Typically, a hidden conflict can eat up as much as 50 percent of senior management's time and energy. If you see this happening, you can be reasonably sure a hidden conflict is perpetuating the problem.

— H. William Dettmer, *Goldratt's Theory of Constraints* [8] ▲

Just as group members, managers, and leaders do not view conflict in exactly the same way, not all conflict is precisely the same nor is the term necessarily pejorative. Conflict is a descriptive term—and to the extent that it accurately reveals or reflects a team's reality—teams and managers alike must recognize and understand the different conflict styles they can face.

ANALYZING CONFLICT STYLES

Understanding your own conflict style, your attitudes toward and methods of coping with conflict, can help you improve teamwork performance and help your teammates to be more productive. Most managers have various kinds of assessment data collected over the course of their careers; a team, however, can jointly decide that a new or updated group assessment might be beneficial to its work. Regardless of how teams first approach an issue, experts generally agree that ignoring or avoiding conflict is the least effective management technique.[9]

While many teams experience episodic conflict that varies from mild to disruptive during a team's life cycle, most are unlikely to need formal mediation or arbitration by a third party—particularly if they take early precautions. Conflicts requiring professional mediation are really of a different kind, rather than degree, of communication barrier. These conflicts may indicate a more serious internal problem with organizational behavior (cultural attitudes, illegal or unethical actions, and so on). Any team or organization needing vigorous conflict resolution strategies are better left to mediation experts. Similarly, management legal teams should work with diplomats and federal agents to negotiate extreme and illegal demands, such as those involving international terrorists, kidnappings, or other violent acts. Sixty percent of *Fortune 500* companies now carry ransom insurance, and firms conducting business in countries with a tenuous relationship with the United States obviously face greater risks. A team—or an organization, for that matter—requiring this kind of external intervention or arbitration is clearly beyond the scope of this book. Our intention here is to improve performance through effective communication skills or strategies.

That said, teams should begin by determining how they will deal with potential conflict up front. While new teams may need to start from ground zero, other groups (particularly those across functions or disciplines) can collect data during the TeamComm assessment stage. A team made up of United Nations' delegates, for example, has very different cultural needs and traditions as opposed to an internal team at FedEx.

The good news is that many organizational conflict strategies for teams share remarkably similar basic features, although some are more complex than others. The variances generally depend on the organizational culture, language, environment, and people involved. Just as organizations shape how, why, and when it is appropriate to use teams, so too must teams customize the appropriate way to manage conflict. If TeamComm strategies are in place, a team is positioned better to embrace a process for conflict management that provides a good fit for its context and discipline. Let's look at some of the options.

One popular instrument is the Thomas-Kilmann Conflict Mode Instrument,[10] which identifies five now-familiar conflict styles: competing, accommodating, avoiding, collaborating, and compromising. The instrument also places these general conflict tendencies on a matrix of opposing dimensions of conflict: concern for self (assertiveness) and concern for others (cooperativeness). To summarize briefly: The competing style is assertive and uncooperative, accommodating is unassertive and cooperative, avoiding is unassertive and uncooperative, collaborating is both assertive and cooperative, and compromising is intermediate in both assertiveness and cooperativeness.

Many others have drawn extensively on the Thomas-Kilmann instrument, reshaping these fundamental distinctions to more complex organizational needs. Rahim and Bonoma, for example, identify five similar conflict styles in their model. They distinguish them according to each style's proportion of concern for self as opposed to concern for others: integrating (high concern for both), dominating (high concern for self and low concern for others), obliging (low concern for self and high concern for others), avoiding (low concern for both self and others), and compromising (moderate levels of concern for both self and others).[11] Examining 1200 corporate managers across the United States, Rahim and Bonoma used a taxonomy that included other organizational variables, such as organizational position, organizational climate, job burnout, job satisfaction, gender, and education.

Sometimes managers fail to recognize that their assessment of the causes, the intensity, or the significance of conflict episodes may be less important than their employees' perceptions of those assessments. Similarly, teams can also fail to acknowledge how differently individual members perceive conflict styles and effective conflict management. Teams must clearly and openly address specific behaviors and potential perceptions of those behaviors. By defining, discussing, and contrasting individual conflict scenarios, teams have an opportunity to distinguish between healthy disagreement and inappropriate conflict behavior.

Identifying individual and organizational competencies is perhaps the newest trend for companies, whether targeting improved managerial recruitment or enhancing team performance.[12] Competency models associate specific conflict styles with appropriate and effective communication in management settings. What is interesting for teams about this ongoing work on conflict is the conclusion that some conflict styles may be preferable to others in managerial and group contexts, marking a departure from the current literature on management and leadership styles. To put it another way, the more effectively a team manages conflict, the more its members will perceive one another as being effective. According to Michael Gross and Laura Guerrero, "The competence model of conflict focuses on three dimensions of competent communication: effectiveness, relational appropriateness, and situational appropriateness. . . . The more effective and appropriate an organizational member is perceived to be during a conflict situation, the more competent he or she will be judged."[13] At the very least, others judge such teams with superior communication skills as being more successful.

Negotiation expert Leigh Thompson also says that managers should correctly diagnose whether they face negative or positive types of conflict. **Emotional conflict,** or Type-A, is personal, defensive, and resentful. Rooted in anger, personal friction, personality clashes, ego, and tension, Type-A is obviously undesirable, with negative consequences for the team. **Cognitive conflict,** or Type-C, on the other hand, is largely depersonalized. It consists of argumentation about the merits of ideas, plans, and projects. Cognitive conflict is often effective in stimulating creativity because it forces people to rethink problems and arrive at outcomes that everyone can live with. Encouraging divergent views in a team, then, benefits creativity and innovation. According to Professor Thompson, "When a majority of members in a team is confronted by the differing opinions of minorities, the majority is forced to think about why the minority disagrees. This thought process could instigate novel ideas."[14]

As a general rule, Type-A Conflict threatens team productivity and cohesion, while Type-C Conflict is thought to benefit team functioning. Why is Type-A Conflict bad for teams? Affective or emotionally based conflict involves thought processes that are largely nonrational, that is, based on feelings rather than facts. When team members are preoccupied with reducing threats, increasing their power, or trying to build team cohesion, they're focusing on each other rather than on the task. In contrast, Type-C Conflict is based largely on facts; the argument is about the merits of the case and not about personality, emotional reactions, or affective responses. If team members focus on the facts at hand and occasionally agree to play devil's advocate in a discussion, they're much more likely to examine all aspects of a problem, particularly those they disagree with and are inclined to overlook or dismiss early in a discussion.[15]

In Karen Jehn's investigation, she found clear evidence for the value of Type-C Conflict while observing six organizational work teams. She looked at everyday conflict among team members over an extended period of time and found that emotional-based conflict (Type-A) was detrimental to two major measures of team productivity: performance and satisfaction. She also found that emotional conflict reduces team effectiveness, whereas groups that accept task-oriented conflict (Type-C) are clearly the most effective. Cognitive conflict was associated with higher-quality decision making, greater understanding, higher commitment levels, and wider acceptance by team members. In contrast, emotional conflict significantly reduced decision quality, understanding, commitment, and acceptance.[16]

These findings make considerable good sense. On the one hand, if your teammates are focused on ideas and issues, the discussion will center more often on whether the team has gathered enough of the proper data, whether the information you have is accurate, and whether the solutions being suggested are likely to succeed. On the other hand, if team members are reacting from an affective vantage point, the discussion can quickly turn personal. Before long, the disagreements aren't about the issues; they're about you and me. If you attack my data (contextual conflict), I won't take it personally; I'll simply check to see if it's accurate. If, however, you attack my personal beliefs (interpersonal conflict), I'm likely to react negatively and in a very nonrational fashion.

IDENTIFYING BEST PRACTICES IN CONFLICT MANAGEMENT

If it is clear that cognitive conflict is healthy (within limits) while affective or emotional conflict is unhealthy for a team, how should team leaders and members respond? What can they do to encourage Type-C Conflict while limiting or eliminating Type-A Conflict? While building on the TeamComm framework provided in Chapter 1, members can head off commonplace sources of conflict through several tactics as discussed next.

REVIEW GROUP OR TEAM GOALS

A shared vision for all team members will make both discussions and decisions about them much easier. In fact, most experts encourage the establishment of vision, values, and beliefs during the formative stages of team-building. With agreement on goals in place, self-centered or emotional responses are much less likely. Teams should also periodically review or reference their assessment forms to clarify direction and perceptions.

REVIEW OR REVISE PROCESSES

The processes by which teams gather information and make decisions are important for managing conflict. If team members know that new ideas must first be put in writing, for example, and then circulated to others in memo format or by e-mail, emotional reactions to informal discussions are much less likely. Team members would know in that instance that a decision about new directions or a change in procedure would be unlikely to occur because none of the team members had taken the initiative to draft ideas or circulate a proposal. Members would view discussions as preliminary and nonbinding. The rules regarding brainstorming are very much the same: suspend judgment, generate as many ideas as possible, then sort through the list by applying agreed-upon values to each suggestion. If a process does not seem to be working, however, it may be time to restructure the effort.

AGREE ON OTHER ISSUES CENTRAL TO TEAM SUCCESS

These matters would include team rewards, team training, and allocation of assets and resources, team activity scheduling, team membership, and team connections with the parent organization. If not all team members understand and agree to the reward scheme, or are forced to train in isolation from other team members, emotional conflict will likely result. If a member schedules a meeting without consulting those affected, other members may feel justified in protesting, "That's not fair." And, if it's not clear to all how people become (or cease to be) members of the team, personalized, emotional reactions are more likely than not.

CREATE A WAY FOR CONFLICT TO SURFACE

Unless members know in advance how and when to express their disagreement, conflict can erupt at almost any time or place. Often, such impromptu expressions of disagreement will disrupt meetings called for other purposes, impede work in progress, or embarrass and upset other team members. Successful, harmonious teams know that disagreement can be managed in a healthy way if team members understand the rules regarding the most appropriate times and places for expressing it. Again, establishing these norms during the early stages of team building would be most helpful. However, if your team has overlooked these small but important issues, you can always revisit them, knowing that your aim is to promote more Type-C discussion.

CLARIFY CULTURAL DIFFERENCES

In groups and teams, competition can arise if management links compensation and rewards to individual, rather than to group performance. This presents an even more complex issue for groups and teams if members' cultural values are somehow different. Teams must collectively agree on how to balance the human need for individual recognition with the goals of the group. In Eastern cultures, for example, where people place greater value on group achievement, intragroup conflict is far less likely to disrupt group processes or interfere with the achievement of group or team goals. For them, it is one team, one achievement, one reward for all.

If teams have worked through the cultural level of the TeamComm model, they may only need to revisit their team values chart (**Assessment Form #6**) or schedule a meeting to refresh memories on differences. If the conflict is severe or escalates too quickly, teams may need a more formal procedure.

Team Quote ▼

Diversity is one of the keys to a successful team. But I'm sure that on every good team, a member has gone home at the end of a day thinking, "this isn't going to work." So my advice is this: Bring in a facilitator. Someone from the outside—an unbiased third party—may have insights about what's working, what's not, and why you are just too close to the project to see clearly. A facilitator may be just what team members need to make the most of their diversity and to help them overcome any personal agendas or conflicts.

— Janine Bay, Director of Vehicle Personalization, Automotive Consumer Services,
Ford Motor Company[17] ▲

Most organizations use some type of problem-solving process to manage formal grievances, but team conflict usually requires a negotiated structure. When East meets West, for example, the possibilities for misunderstanding, misinterpretation, and misrepresentation because of differences in communication style, attitudes toward conflict, and translating the causes and responsibility for that conflict can take on significant consequences. While the eleven days during which U.S. naval aviators were held in China during the 2001 spy plane incident did not shake the world, diplomatic relations were disrupted, and progress toward other U.S.–Chinese goals was diminished. The specific language of relatively simple messages between two major powers captured the world's attention as experts debated the meaning and the implications of a simple word, *apology*. In the course of the negotiations, expressed *regrets* became *sincere regrets* and *sorry* became *very sorry,* but both countries still disagree about what those words actually meant.

The lesson is, the more complex the organization, the more complex the issues. Eliyahu M. Goldratt's Theory of Constraints provides a comprehensive and highly structured tool for conflict resolution within his systems improvement philosophy. Differing from other continuous improvement methods by emphasizing the interdependence among system processes, Goldratt's view of systems as "networks of chains" also fits together nicely with TeamComm strategies. William Dettmer's analysis of Goldratt's theory provides an excellent guide to the logical tools of the Thinking Process, first by explaining the five focusing steps involved in the Theory of Constraints and then applying them to organizational examples illustrating different component interactions.[18] Goldratt's system of logical tools uses decision trees for managing operations, addressing everything from what to change and how to change it by managing the "weakest link" in the chain (system). The Conflict Resolution Diagram (the "evaporating cloud") resolves conflicts that hinder a system's optimal performance by identifying invalid assumptions. Once identified and invalidated, these assumptions lead to ideas that provide solutions.

While Goldratt's diagram may be too elaborate a structure for some, using **decision trees**— visual depictions of a process—is a common organizational strategy for solving difficult problems, particularly those involving competing or conflicting interests. In fact, the advantage of using Decision Tree Analysis[19] is precisely its formal, objective process for determining difficult courses of action through a series of logical steps:

1. Depict the decisions to be made and possible outcomes for each decision.
2. Assign probabilities to each of the uncertain events.
3. Assign values to each of the possible outcomes.
4. Calculate the expected values for each possible alternative.
5. Identify soft factors that are relevant to the decisions to be made.
6. Decide on the best alternative.[20]

Such a process has drawbacks, of course; an overly complicated approach is not appropriate for relatively clear, straightforward differences of opinion (interpersonal conflict) or in interpretation (contextual conflict). Moreover, such a model assumes that those involved have complete information and are rational people who will all recognize the same sequence of steps as being logical.

As we all know, however, teams, like individual decision makers, rarely have all the information they need at the right time and are composed of individuals who may or may not see things the same way. And, just as no conflict episodes are ever exactly the same, not all team members will agree on a perfect approach to their situation. If they can agree on one that's appropriate, that should be enough. The point is this: A team ultimately sets its own methods. The more disciplined the team, the more effectively the members will communicate about and manage conflict. A team using TeamComm strategies, for example, is already accustomed to a disciplined process—the kind of discipline necessary to handle most forms of short-term conflict. In most cases, a simple tactic will be sufficient as long as it's clearly understood and agreed to by everyone on the team.

PREDICTING REASONS TEAMS FAIL

The essence of teams, according to Professors Carl Larson and Frank LaFasto of the University of Denver, is teamwork. That may seem self-evident, but it's worth exploring. "If a team is a group of people pursuing a specific performance objective, the achievement of which requires coordinated action, then teamwork must be a significant factor in determining a team's success," they write.[21] Teamwork, however, implies that the outcome—the team's performance or achievement of its goals—will somehow produce results that exceed the individual abilities of its members, even its very best members. Teams are formed, remember, to produce synergistic outcomes. Although widely overused and sometimes misapplied, synergy still applies to teams that create a whole greater than the sum of its parts, or a result greater than any member can achieve alone.

As we learned in Chapter 1, teams occasionally fall short of our expectations for them. Some even manage to perform suboptimally for extended periods. Consider the Chicago Cubs, for example. The team members are all professional athletes of considerable skill, some of them with exceptional individual abilities. Yet, season after season since 1908, the Chicago National League Baseball Club (as it is officially known) has underachieved—this, in spite of a financially solvent owner, the Tribune Company of Chicago; capable management; and a wonderful ballpark in which to play. By the conclusion of the 2000 season, the Cubs had fallen to last place in the National League's Central Division, nearly thirty games behind the divisional leader.

Why do teams fail? What can go wrong (aside from perennial difficulty with relief pitching)? Regardless of the profession or industry, one answer seems to be poor communication among teams of individuals. The healthcare industry provides a disturbing and vivid example. *NBC Nightly News* reported on April 24, 2001, that a nine-month-old baby died because of an overdose of morphine. The reason for the mistake, apparently, was that the transcribed order was for .5 mg, but the clerk read the order as 5 mg. Similarly, a recent *New York Times* article cites several horrifying cases of wrong-site surgery over the last year. According to the article, hundreds of cases occur every year in the United States and are increasing. In 1999, The Institute of Medicine of the National Academy of Sciences reported that medical errors kill between 44,000 and 98,000 hospitalized patients a year.[23]

"The problem," says Dr. Elise Becher, assistant professor of pediatrics and health policy at Mount Sinai School of Medicine, who has researched the occurrences of and causes for such errors, "is usually not an individual person making a mistake. It is individuals making several mistakes, and systems not preventing those mistakes from doing harm. Latent conditions for these mistakes," Becher explains, "include holes in presurgical procedures and problems with the way staff members communicate during an operation." A required number of people should verify that the correct limb, as well as the correct person, has been prepared for surgery. "Things should be reviewed by an entire team," and "there should be constant checking and discussion."[24]

Other conditions, which Becher calls "environmental," include staff shortages and subspecialization. The trend among doctors to choose a narrow specialty and to focus on one body part, rather than the entire patient, results in the patient seeing several specialists (a gastroenterologist, a urologist, and a surgeon, for example), but no one checking the whole system. Such practices "decrease the likelihood that a patient will be surrounded by caregivers who actually know the patient." One study by the Joint Commission on Accreditation of Healthcare Organizations cited fifteen wrong-site surgery cases all to have several common factors, including the involvement of more than one surgeon, the performance of several different procedures during one surgery, and pressure from hospital administrators on surgical teams to speed things up.[25]

Team Quote ▼

We try to keep the team together as we move into development. I like to think of a baseball team. Some players come and go, but the team culture stays the same.

— Paul Horn, IBM[22] ▲

Perhaps the most disturbing news, however, is that surgery is not a culture that embraces teamwork or questions from subordinates. *The British Medical Journal* reported that only 55% of surgeons disagreed with the statement that junior team members should not question decisions made by senior members. More revealing, while 64% of surgeons surveyed felt that high levels of teamwork occurred in their operation room, only 28% of surgical nurses shared that view and only 39% of anesthesiologists, "underscoring a strong disconnect" among the different team members "whose functions are critical to successful surgery."[26]

Medical mistakes can result from a deadly combination of errors, dramatically illustrating the range of possible miscommunication errors among teams. More broadly speaking, serious difficulties for team communication—across industries and professional disciplines—seem to fall into seven separate categories.

COMMON-KNOWLEDGE EFFECT

Among the most beneficial aspects of belonging to a team is the opportunity to share information that only team members know and understand. Sharing unique information can be especially valuable to team members as they decide on additional information to gather and next steps to take in achieving their goals. Unfortunately, that's not how most teams operate—at least not initially. Many teams revisit information already well known to team members, review decisions already made, and rehash discussions that have already taken place within the group. Teams tend to discuss what everyone already knows. Gigone and Hastie,[27] social psychologists who have researched team information sharing and performance, call this the "common knowledge effect." They also found that information that is widely known by group members in advance of a group decision tends to have a disproportionately important effect on their decisions. This finding would argue in favor of group members sharing as much information as possible, as far in advance of a decision as possible, so that group members don't overlook or discount important knowledge, simply because it's new and, perhaps, not well understood.

FALSE CONSENSUS EFFECT

This phenomenon is sometimes referred to as The Abilene Paradox, made famous by management theorist Jerry Harvey.[28] Rather than sit around the house, drink lemonade and play dominoes on a scorching Sunday afternoon in west Texas, someone suggests that the Harvey family all get in the unair-conditioned 1958 Buick and drive to a cafeteria fifty-three miles away in Abilene. Everyone agrees, not because anyone really wants to drive through a blinding dust storm in intolerably hot temperatures to the cafeteria in Abilene, but to be agreeable. They put up with a choice they clearly do not favor in order to avoid confrontation. According to Harvey, this behavior is a form of pluralistic ignorance; group members adopt a position because they feel other members want it, or because they don't want to challenge one another. In other words, they'll suffer through a 106-mile roundtrip in the heat to a restaurant they don't want to eat in, just to achieve consensus. The irony of this is that many groups and teams have very little difficulty managing honest, open disagreement. It's the management of agreement they can't seem to handle.

Why would otherwise sensible, intelligent people agree to something they really don't want to do? Is the desire for consensus and harmony so powerful that it can lead a group to a decision that's unpopular or unsound? In general, group members will go along with others in the group if they feel intimidated or unable to influence the outcome of the decision. Studies often refer to such views as **self-limiting behavior.** In a survey of more than 500 managers in 1996, Mulvey, Veiga, and Elsass[29] identify six possible causes of such behavior:

The presence of someone with expertise. If a person with greater apparent expertise in the subject of the group's decision is present, many members will limit their own behavior to agreement, either because they don't want to reveal their own lack of expertise, or because they don't want to be a source of conflict.

The presentation of a compelling argument. If someone offers a coherent argument at an appropriate moment in a group's deliberation, group members can often feel compelled to go along, even if they disagree. Without an equally compelling counterargument available, members may feel powerless to sway group opinion.

A lack of confidence in one's ability to contribute. Team members who feel unsure of their own expertise or their ability to offer meaningful insight into the decision process may simply hold back or keep quiet during discussion.

An unimportant or meaningless decision. If the group decision is not seen as especially important or meaningful to all group members, many may simply say, "Who cares?" and allow others who think the issue is important to influence the outcome.

Pressure from others to conform to the team's decision. Influence can come in the form of rank, authority, status, expertise, or force of personality. And, unless group members are both willing and able to resist pressure from dominant or assertive group members, they're likely to go along with whatever decision seems most palatable to the majority.

A dysfunctional decision-making climate. Group members may engage in self-limiting behavior if they perceive the decision-making processes to be untrustworthy, unreliable, disorganized, or frustrating in some other important dimension. Rather than try to take on a hopeless cause, group members may simply say, "It's their problem. I don't really care what they decide."[30]

IN-GROUP BIAS

This is a subtle but very real form of prejudice in which group and team members come to believe they are better than those who are not part of their group. Cultural anthropologists see this behavior as a form of ethnocentrism in which members view the norms, values, and practices of the group as inherently superior to those of outsiders.[31] Such views can be particularly harmful when the group must interact with other groups—in collaborative or cooperative activities—or assimilate new members, as in a corporate merger or acquisition.

OUT-GROUP HOMOGENEITY

As members of a group or team work and interact with one another, they come to know and understand the differences that separate them. They may also develop stereotypes or homogeneous images of those who are not members of the group. Stereotyping is ascribing to all members of a group or class those characteristics or behaviors observed in one or a few. The very processes that permit group members to bond with one another may encourage them to see outsiders not only as different from their group but also as very similar to one another. In extreme circumstances, an us versus them mentality may arise in which group members begin to think "It's us against the world."[32]

TRANSACTIVE MEMORY

As good as the human information-processing system is, according to Leigh Thompson, it is insufficient for most organizational work. As a result, people often rely on others for the information they need to perform complex tasks. **Transactive memory** is essentially a group-level information-processing system designed to pay attention to, encode, store, process, and retrieve information.[33] This way of thinking becomes a kind of group memory, but one that is specialized in some important ways. Each group, for example, has its experts and specialists—people who pay attention to particular kinds of information and who remember particular details. The group as a whole knows, more or less, what it is that others in the group know, though each member clearly knows something slightly different from the others. They also rely on individuals within the group to be responsible for specialized fragments of knowledge. The advantage of transactive memory is that groups can collectively attend to and remember much more information than any one individual possibly could. The disadvantage is that team members come to depend on one another for information that may become crucial to team activities and decisions. When key members of the team fail to attend to, process, or remember such information, the entire team is threatened, for if those members fail to share what they know with the team in a timely or appropriate fashion, conflict may result.

SOCIAL COHESION

People belong to groups and teams for a variety of reasons. Some seek out membership because of the social, financial, or professional benefits it may confer. Others, involuntarily assigned by a supervisor to a work group, may have neither a sense of commitment nor a real understanding of the roles and expectations of other group members. Socially cohesive groups tend to function at much higher levels of productivity than groups that are not cohesive. In other words, people who get along and both appreciate and enjoy their group or team roles more will probably achieve their collective goals more quickly and efficiently. Groups hang together for a number of reasons: shared values, agreement on goals and objectives, external social pressure, common cultural norms or practices, and—not surprisingly—personal compatibility. Teams that fail to develop a sense of social cohesion will experience greater levels of dysfunctional conflict and, in all likelihood, fail to achieve the goals they've set for themselves or which have been set for them by a parent organization. The lesson for team members and leaders is obvious: Time and effort spent developing group cohesion or team spirit is time and energy that will not be spent trying to resolve emotional conflict or noncognitive disagreement.

ETHICAL DILEMMAS

What do you do if you disagree substantively with your team's or your organization's policies, methods, or new directions because of fundamental ethical differences? While experts disagree as to the frequency of such instances, many offer similar observations about individual values: "If you are attached to almost any group, you will find some things internal to the group that are distasteful," says Robert P. Lawry, law professor and director of the Center for Professional Ethics at Case Western Reserve University in Cleveland.[34] Linda Klebe Trevino, a professor of organizational behavior at The Pennsylvania State University, observes, "It's a mythology that there are all these autonomous principled thinkers walking around organizations. It's just not true." Joseph L. Badaracco, Jr., business ethics professor at Harvard Business School, agrees:

"Most companies and most executives really look for the middle of the road and try to stay away from controversy."[35]

If, however, an employee can't change an unacceptable and critical difference, it's best to leave, says Badaracco: "People aren't very effective as thorns. Unless one can accept the situation or hope to change it, there is no point sticking around and becoming more agitated." "If your values clash with your organization's," Seglin concludes, "and you have previously made it clear that, being the person of principle that you are, you would never stand for such policies or behavior, then you should leave. You should go not because it is unethical to stay, but because your integrity depends on it."[36]

GETTING AHEAD OF THE CURVE

When team communication breaks down, it rarely involves all of the members at the same time. Interpersonal conflicts, misunderstandings, language barriers, or differences in management or learning styles are the usual culprits for difficulties during team performance. If the work processes have been clear and agreed to through consensus or through some other method, members may only need to regroup and refresh collective memories. If, however, members have relied on a tacit understanding that all members have similar work habits and disciplines or even a spoken pledge that "We'll all give 100%," a team can quickly find its performance less than synergetic and soon spiraling downward.

Recalling the TeamComm systems model, potential barriers can pop up at any level: self, group, institution, culture, or technology. The key to overcoming any of them, and preventing them from developing into unhealthy conflict or even insurmountable obstacles, is to match the level where the problem exists with an appropriate communication strategy for that level. For example, let's say two teammates have trouble agreeing on a marketing premise. No matter what the product or where they work, the team needs to get the issue out on the table as soon as possible. If either team member goes privately to a supervisor or happens to mention it at a luncheon meeting of division heads, the problem will not go away. It may actually worsen because an institutional approach is ineffective for an interpersonal issue. Similarly, if two other teammates suddenly find themselves with opposing views of market segmentation in Mexico, the solution probably lies at the cultural level. Rather than saying, "You're wrong," both should redirect their focus by researching and supplying new data.

Today, most workplace barriers that can impair communication arise from several commonalities. These do not necessarily result in conflict, but they can certainly create sparks in a volatile atmosphere, where employees are chronically overworked, overscheduled, and overwhelmed. For teams to get ahead of the curve means not only being attuned to these daily realities but taking measures to overcome barriers and firewalls before they are too firmly entrenched.

MULTITASKING

Few of us escape multitasking at work. In fact, we've gotten so good at it that we practice it almost continuously. If communication is by phone, do members focus on the team issue put before them or continue to work on an individual task while also considering suggestions for the team? If the team is working together online, which takes priority: the group discussion or the individual, mental list of projects still pending for the day?

Reestablishing the skill of a single focus improves team communication simply by eliminating interference from other mental activities. Retraining ourselves to concentrate on one issue at a time can produce meetings that are more efficient and discussions that can help clarify consensus action. Compelling evidence now exists that multitasking also wastes time. University of Michigan researchers and the Federal Aviation Administration found that humans lose time when switching from tasks of varying complexity and familiarity; the greater the task complexity, the greater the time cost. According to investigator David Meyer, "For each aspect of human performance—perceiving, thinking, and acting—people have specific mental resources whose effective use requires supervision through executive mental control."[37]

MAINTAINING TRUST

The need for trust is absolute and requires ongoing nurturing. Uncertainty undermines any team effort. Members uncertain of one another's motives or actions are less likely to share openly with the team. Any new development, rumor, or misread e-mail can spark a potential controversy or even undo an established (or assumed) climate of trust. As such incidents emerge, members should make sure they confront them with dispatch and work at maintaining trust throughout the team contract.

ADJUSTING FOR PACE

Although the institutional climate affects the work pace generally, individual work paces vary, and each individual must communicate that pace effectively to others. A redline message (flagged for urgency) signals to the recipient the need for an immediate response. If the receiver perceives the issue differently after reading it, he or she may be less conscientiously responsive the next time. After five or six such episodes of urgency, the receiver may develop temporary color blindness to such red flags.

Eventually, speed of technology hits a critical threshold. We may be able to send and receive, compose and edit, revise and correct messages more quickly, but we do not think any faster than we ever could. A good idea still takes time to formulate, develop, analyze, digest, and present before it becomes a strategy, a business plan, or a best practice. Our tendency is to respond as quickly as possible, but given what is possible, we must pace our work accordingly, being vigilant in our use of effective and appropriate communication strategies.

HONORING LEARNING STYLES, COMPETENCIES, AND EXPERIENCES

A failure to appreciate the value of others' attitudes, abilities, cultures, values, and observations that are different from our own may limit the team's vision and performance. Inventories and assessment tools such as the ones introduced here or by others[38] provide useful ways for you to continue your individual learning and improve team processes. Returning to these tools, particularly if conflict arises or confusion begins, can help you and other team members readjust your perceptions and, perhaps, your work habits.

USING E-COMMUNICATION

We are just now beginning to appreciate how different electronic communication really is. Recent work on gender[39] illustrates that men and women not only interact and communicate differently, but that these differences carry over in sometimes unexpected ways in e-mail (as in other interactions). Consequently, women and men are more likely to miscommunicate or misperceive messages online, without the accompanying advantage of nonverbal cues (gestures, facial responses, inflection, eye contact). Online flaming is much more frequent now than it was a few years ago due to pace, impatience, and daily pressures.

E-mail is also a favorite venue for excuses because it disallows skeptical readers to directly question the writer about the validity of the excuse. By emphasizing the view that communication is one-way, we tend to focus on sending more than on receiving. A true exchange of meaning may provoke several replies or reactions taking place over days or weeks, but none in real time.

Ongoing research on teams and diversity continues to extend and refine our understanding of the range of effects these exchanges can have on team performance and evaluation, as well as on team communication among diverse team members. **Asynchronous** e-communication, communication occuring at different times for senders and receivers, is the most likely to produce problems (and also the most difficult to study). Understanding is not synchronous; nor is misunderstanding. Teams cannot regulate when understanding takes place any more than they can regulate ideas or retrieve a message that ignites sparks. By the time the sender smells the smoke, her original intent may be in ashes, and damage control or backtracking to explain may not be an option if the sender never sees or understands the problem.

STRATEGIES FOR EFFECTIVE TEAM COMMUNICATION

What simple conclusions can we glean, finally, for groups and teams?

1. **The kind of team matters.** Each team determines how it will use a model to measure performance, and the kind of team it has become will drive both operational procedures and strategies. Cohen and Bailey suggest using different heuristic models for different kinds of teams to measure performance.[40] While there are notable differences in team functions and processes, however, most TeamComm strategies apply to a broad range of teams, from working groups to top management teams.

2. **Effective TeamComm strategies enhance performance outcomes. Period.** Regardless of what teams call them, a defined set of communication strategies contributes to the processes teams use and the results they generate. The key is to use methods or protocols that are not only flexible enough to withstand market trends, business cycles, management fads, and external forces, but which are also appropriate for the organization, the culture, and the environment in which it operates.

    Warning signs of poor communication can appear quickly if companies, organizations, or teams practice outdated methods without challenging their assumptions and practices in a competitive, dramatically changing world. For those who rely on the familiar, the expedient, or unenlightened practices, extinction may be just around the corner.

3. **Teams that are flexible, adaptive, diverse, interactive, attentive, and responsive communicate most effectively.** Teams require members with diverse communication skills. Effective teams communicate well because they are flexible, adaptive, and diverse. Understanding the communication challenges of the new world in which we live means understanding new opportunities for connecting the old ways in which people think and work together. One such opportunity is the newly described area of knowledge management.

Creating the positions of chief knowledge officer may very well provide another tool for organizations that have yet to successfully implement teams. Those who most need to share knowledge may need some senior-level guidance to get it done.

Knowledge managers—experts who tap into the organization's human resources, identify areas of expertise, and match skills to project management—may offer, ironically, a more traditional approach to teamwork by helping teams help themselves. By using a broad range of communication skills to solve conflicts, to match collaborative expertise with functional purpose, and to audit an organization's resources, knowledge managers offer the skill sets traditionally expected from project or team leaders or chief executives—but without the insider associations.

4. **Communication technologies will continually change communication strategies.** Multicultural communication will continue to blur traditional boundaries and redefine our understanding of diversity. We will also develop new ways to talk about teams—the structures, the processes, and the behaviors. E-communication or e-personal communication will continue to change the way we interact with others. Less face-to-face communication and more telemediation will mean few nonverbal and contextual cues to work from. We will be challenged in such situations to understand not only what people think, but how they feel.

The Internet has only begun to fulfill its potential as a major system of communication, but while we use its present capabilities, we must continuously explore ways to develop its future applications. "The Internet," writes Gary E. Rieschel, "is about communications, and people have never at any time in history stopped wanting to communicate." Rieschel is executive managing director at Softbank Venture Capital, one of the largest backers of Internet ventures.[41] For any industry that relies heavily on the flow of information—financial services, education, healthcare, government, and entertainment—the technology of the Internet has radically changed practices and greatly reduced the cost of that information. The lesson for teams is to use the Internet wisely by instantly accessing archived information and sharing expertise quickly, but not by regarding it as a surrogate team member.

Matching an appropriate strategy with the organizational culture and environment provides the best solution not only for teams but also for businesses. We must learn to embrace the accelerating pace of communication and the changes in delivery technology as energizing and enabling forces in our shared environment. To meet the challenges of a new world effectively, teams must depend on these new forms of communication. Ultimately, however, it is your responsibility to yourself and to your group to set performance standards that are appropriate and meaningful. While those standards may vary, strategies for successful communication are universal and timeless.

In spite of our best efforts or intentions, teams can still face disappointments. Sometimes the reasons are external and beyond our control. But if they're internal, they are often the result of unrealistic expectations. Perhaps the best response to that is to examine the reasons, readjust the focus, and plan for better future efforts. The last section offers a dozen guidelines for your teams that do just that.

SECRETS OF SUCCESS

1. **Exceed expectations:** Go beyond the ordinary response if you want extraordinary results.
2. **Average efforts yield average outcomes:** If you simply meet the requirements, you've simply done your job. Don't expect applause.
3. **Limit distractions:** Good communication is tough under the best circumstances. Outside interference (noise, multitasking, competing agendas and interests, etc.) increases the complexity of tasks and decreases accuracy.
4. **Analyze without obstructing:** If you are trying to solve a problem, offer a solution, rather than ways to avoid it.
5. **Encourage and accept disinterested appraisals, evaluations, and feedback:** Friends often tell us what we want to hear or what they are comfortable saying.
6. **Recognize and acknowledge superior efforts:** This applies particularly if the efforts aren't your own.
7. **Don't shoot the messenger:** If your efforts aren't always rewarded the way you would prefer, try not to blame those who fail to recognize your brilliance.
8. **Take disappointments in stride:** Readjust for failures and try to repeat successes.
9. **Practice:** Focus on one skill that you need to improve until you get results.
10. **Don't disappoint others:** This is the best way to avoid disappointing yourself.
11. **Improve your own memory:** Do this before you question others' perceptions.
12. **Differences matter, and so do similarities:** Gender matters. Race matters. Culture matters. Ethnicity matters. Disability matters. Religion matters. In short, people matter the most.

DISCUSSION QUESTIONS

1. What is your conflict style?

2. What styles are represented on your team?

3. Review the headlines in today's *Wall Street Journal*. What evidence of conflict do you find brewing within or between companies or organizations? Choose one topic with your team and track the development of the conflict through online resources. In individual memos, identify the major players and the reasons for the conflict. Provide an analysis of what you believe to be the critical issues, and provide evidence for your views. Discuss and compare your analysis with your teammates' responses.

ENDNOTES

1. *http://www.bemorecreative.com*
2. K. Boulding, *Conflict and Defense* (New York: Harper Row, 1963).
3. Karen Jehn and Elizabeth A. Mannix, "The Dynamic Nature of Conflict: A Longitudinal Study of Intragroup Conflict and Group Performance," *Academy of Management Journal,* 44, no. 2 (April 2000), 239. Jehn and Mannix cite a number of other studies: A. Amason and H. Sapienza, "The Effects of Top Management Team Size and Interaction Norms on Cognitive and Affective Conflict," *Journal of Management,* 23, no. 4 (1997): 495–516; R. Cosier and G. Rose, "Cognitive Conflict and Goal Conflict Effects on Task Performance," *Organizational Behavior and Human Performance* 19 (1977): 378–391; H. Guetzkow and J. Gyr, "An Analysis of Conflict in Decision Making Groups," *Human Relations* 7 (1954): 367–381; K. Jehn, "The Impact of Intragroup Conflict on Effectiveness: A Multimethod Examination of the Benefits and Detriments of Conflict." Unpublished doctoral dissertation, Northwestern University Graduate School of Management, Evanston, IL, 1992; L. Pelled, "Demographic Diversity, Conflict, and Work Group Outcomes: An Intervening Process Theory," *Organization Science* 7, no. 6 (1996): 615–631.
4. Jehn and Mannix, 239.
5. Amason and Sapienza.
6. Jehn and Mannix.
7. Steve Hamm, "Less Ego, More Success," *BusinessWeek,* July 23, 2001, 59.
8. H. William Dettmer, *Goldratt's Theory of Constraints: A Systems Approach to Continuous Improvement* (Milwaukee, WI: ASQC, 1997), 126.
9. Thomas-Kilmann Conflict Mode Instrument, 1974. See Appendix A for a list of assessment tools and organizational instruments.
10. Ibid.
11. See, for example, A. M. Nicotera, ed., *Conflict and Organizations: Communicative Processes* (Albany, NY: State University of New York Press, 1995).
12. Michael A. Gross and Laura K. Guerrero, "Managing Conflict Appropriately and Effectively: An Application of the Competence Model to Rahim's Organizational Conflict Styles," *International Journal of Conflict Management,* 11, no. 3 (2000): 201.
13. Ibid.
14. Leigh Thompson, *Making the Team: A Guide for Managers* (Upper Saddle River, NJ: Prentice-Hall, 2000), 217–218.
15. Ibid.
16. Karen A. Jehn, "Enhancing Effectiveness: An Investigation of Advantages and Disadvantages of Value-Based Intragroup Conflict," *International Journal of Conflict Management* 5, no. 3 (July 1994): 223–238.
17. Regina Maruca, "What Makes Teams Work?" *Fast Company,* November 2000.
18. Dettmer.
19. See, for example, Allan Edward Barsky, *Conflict Resolution for the Helping Professions* (Belmont, CA: Brooks/Cole, 2000), 293–300.
20. Ibid.
21. C. E. Larson and Frank M. J. LaFasto, *Team Work: What Must Go Right/What Can Go Wrong* (Newbury Park, CA: Sage, 1989), 84.
22. As quoted in William J. Holstein, "How Big Blue Plays D," *Business 2.0,* August/September 2001, 154.
23. "So the Tumor's in the Left Brain, Right?" *The New York Times,* April 1, 2001, A-23.
24. Ibid. All citations to Dr. Belcher appear in the *Times* article.
25. Ibid. The study cited in the *Times* article is "Error, Stress, and Teamwork in Medicine and Aviation: Cross Sectional Surveys," J. Bryon Sexton, Eric J. Thomas, and Robert L. Helmneich, *British Medical Journal* (2000), 320:745–749.

26. Ibid.

27. D. Gigone and R. Hastie, "The Common Knowledge Effect: Information Sharing and Group Judgment," *Journal of Personality and Social Psychology* 72, no. 1 (1993): 132–140.

28. Jerry Harvey, "The Abilene Paradox: The Management of Agreement," *Organizational Dynamics* 1, no. 3 (1974): 63–80.

29. P. W. Mulvey, J. F. Veiga, and P. M. Elsass, "When Teammates Raise a White Flag," *Academy of Management Executive* 10, no. 1 (1996): 40–49.

30. Ibid.

31. M. P. Orbe and T. M. Harris, *Interracial Communication: Theory into Practice* (Belmont, CA: Wadsworth/Thomson Learning, 2001), 7.

32. Thompson.

33. D. M. Wegner, "Transactive Memory: A Contemporary Analysis of the Group Mind," in *Theories of Group Behavior,* ed. B. Mullen and G. Goethals. (New York: Springer-Verlag, 1986), 185–208.

34. As quoted in Jeffrey Seglin, "When to Go Along, and When to walk Away," *The New York Times,* February 18, 2001, 4BU.

35. Ibid.

36. Ibid. Today an increasing number of organizations are set up to assist investors and employees concerned about social responsibility issues, which can cover product and environmental practices, as well as oppressive governments. **The Franklin Research and Development Institute** has substantial information on financial issues of companies as well as corporate management. **The Investor Responsibility Research Center,** set up by universities and foundations, serves as an alternate source of information to major institutional investors as a response to shareholder activists. **New Consumer** works with the US-based Council on Economic priorities to identify "better practices" and works on corporate social responsibility issues and consumerism. In addition, two other organizations help coordinate individual investors concerned about social responsibility: the **Ethical Investment Research Service Ltd.** and the **Social Investment Forum.**

37. For information, see these online sources: *http://www.frdc.com.* Contact: Simon Billenness; *mkt@irrc.org*; *info@socialinvest.org.*

38. See Appendix A. David Kolb's Model of Experiential Learning and Inventory of Learning Styles provides a useful way for groups to begin their discussions of individual learning and team processes. For a comparison of research approaches to learning styles, see Charles S. Claxton and Patricia H. Murrell, *Learning Styles,* no. 4, Ashe-Eric Higher Education Report Series, 1987.

39. Kristin Daly and Herminia Ibarra, "Gender Differences in Managerial Behavior: The Ongoing Debate," Harvard Business School 9-494-038, March 12, 1995; Gefen and Straub, "Gender Differences in the Perception and Use of E-mail: An Extension to the Technology Acceptance Model," *MIS Quarterly* 21, no. 1 (1997): 389–400; Deborah Tannen, "The Power of Talk: Who Gets Heard and Why," *Harvard Business Review,* September–October, 1995, 138–48.

40. Cohen and Bailey, 281.

41. Gary E. Rieschel, Executive Managing Director at Softbank Venture Capital, as quoted in *BusinessWeek,* March 26, 2001, 118.

For many years, Fisher Brothers has been one of America's preeminent real estate development and investment companies. When the company and its business partners needed to finance a prestigious New York office property, they turned to Union Bank of Switzerland.

Despite an unfavorable market that had not seen a single-asset office securitization completed in years, the UBS team of specialists structured and placed $265 million in debt. The deal structure gave Fisher Brothers access to low-cost capital with interest rate protection, while satisfying European investor demand for floating rate paper. How was Union Bank of Switzerland able to turn a complex financial challenge into a successful transaction? The answer, in part, is team communication, according to Tiffanie Fisher of the UBS Securities Real Estate Group. An important component of that process meant managing team conflict, as well.

Ms. Fisher, who is no relation to the client in this transaction, helped to form a small team of bankers and real estate specialists to deal with the challenge of restructuring the debt. "Fisher Brothers has been among our largest private banking clients for the past ten years," she observed, "so it was natural for them to come to us for help." But this was a risky, complex deal. "The client owned a 50-story, upscale office tower in mid-town Manhattan," she explained. "The building had considerable debt. Some $400 million was maturing and much of that debt had been based on projected revenues rather than actual cash flow."

"Please understand," she explained, "office buildings are much higher risk for refinancing, because with *any* downturn in the economy, a client's tenants and income can go away in a hurry. Even prestigious office space can be very turbulent." What could Union Bank do for its long-time private banking client? "In May of 1995, three officers from Fisher Brothers came to us and explained the dilemma. We decided to form a small team of three specialists, headed by Tom Curtin of our Real Estate Group." With just three team members from each organization, communication at first was simple. "If we had a question," said Ms. Fisher, "we'd just pick up the phone and call or, on occasion, arrange for a meeting."

As the teams grew in size, though, so did their communication problems. "In the summer of 1995, we began adding specialists to the team," she said. "We needed a lawyer, an investment banker, industry specialists, and so on. And because real estate is a very different industry from others, we had to make sure each team member shared a common vocabulary—a language we could comfortably use with one another." And, while most communication within the team went smoothly, the process was not conflict-free.

"Industry specialists have their point of view," said Ms. Fisher. "The investment bankers have theirs. And, of course, almost no one sees things the way the attorneys do. What sort of conflict arose? "Sometimes it would be priorities. On other occasions, it would be tempo. The brokers wanted to move quickly to take advantage of shifting market conditions, but the lawyers were always urging us to move more deliberately." How did the team prevent such disagreement from unraveling the deal? "We simply agreed, up front, that we would not let this become personal. We agreed to put our hopes and fears aside and let the facts and the experts do the talking." Ultimately, she said, it worked well because all team members were in complete agreement on their goals. "We knew what we wanted," she said. "At first, we weren't sure how we would get there, but we did agree to remain patient and good humored."

Separate communication problems arose as the bank asked for more financial data from their client, Fisher Brothers. "Privately-owned firms just don't record and report data in the same way publicly-held firms do," she explained. "With some companies we honestly have to explain, step-by-step what sort of information we need, and what form we'll need it in."

Confidentiality issues can also complicate a deal. "We interact frequently with outside agencies," Ms. Fisher said, "including rating agencies such as Standard and Poor's. We also talk regularly to law firms, engineers and others outside the immediate circle. With a lawyer, client confidentiality is assumed. But with other experts and specialists," she observed, "we require non-disclosure agreements. And we had to talk with one another frequently to make sure we each knew what we could say and to whom we could say it. And, of course," she added, "if we ever represent competitors in a deal, we're required to set up what's called a 'Chinese Wall,' an internal barrier through which absolutely no information can pass."

As Ms. Fisher's team at Union Bank grew, she observed some important changes in the way they communicated—with each other and with the client. "We began as generalists," she said, "taking a very big-picture view of the deal. Even though we each came from a specialized background in the bank, we talked and thought about all aspects of the re-structuring." By winter of 1996, the deal was far enough along to permit team members to work exclusively on their own special areas. "We eventually moved back into our functional areas," she noted. "As we accomplished more, we worked as a team less and less. So, our focus moved from macro to micro over the course of a year."

Any other complications for this team? "Well," she said, "even though we live and work in New York, Union Bank has a very European culture. We're hierarchically organized; titles and degrees are important. Rank and status are important. We don't ignore those things here, but working on a small team gave us a chance to work around many of those issues. There are hierarchical protocols to honor," she explained, "but in the early stages of team formation, we agreed that we could work a bit less formally and get more done." What did that mean for communication? "Well," she said, "Richard Fisher felt he could call me directly on some issues, rather than having to talk to my supervisor first. In ordinary, day-to-day banking transactions, that wouldn't happen."

Any lessons from the Fisher Brothers–Union Bank deal? "I found," said Ms. Fisher, "that as the team learned more, I learned more. I benefited directly from the learning curve of my teammates. In other organizational structures, that doesn't happen. We focus on our own specialties and tend to repeat the same lessons over and over."

Any observations regarding conflict during all of this? "People of good will can work together, but it's not as simple as agreeing to 'get along,'" she said. "Eventually various financial positions will come into conflict and we have to decide what's best for the client. If we can't agree on that, we can't represent them effectively.

In retrospect, I think, knowing that the client was counting on us made a big difference to us. Their goals became our goals."

Source: O'Hair, Dan; O'Rourke, James S.; and O'Hair, Mary John. *Business Communication: A Framework for Success* (Cincinnati, OH: South-Western College Publishing, 2001), 501–502.

QUESTIONS

1. Assuming you were in Ms. Fisher's position when the client approached Union Bank of Switzerland, what would you want to know before agreeing to take on the refinancing of his office building? Where would you get such information?

2. How important do you think it is for members of a team to work in the same location? Should all of you be in the same office? On the same floor? In the same building?

3. How often would team members need to communicate with one another to set up and close a restructuring deal such as the one the Fisher Brothers were hoping for?

4. How important would you regard face-to-face meetings with your own team members? How about meetings with your client?

5. How comfortable would you feel in calling or speaking directly with a client or member of your own organization who is both older and higher in rank? What could you do to increase your comfort level—and that of the client—in dealing with issues such as age, rank, status, and seniority?

6. What can teams do to increase the quality and rate of learning they experience? What would you suggest to Ms. Fisher as she forms another team to finance the bank's next major real estate deal?

7. What's the value, from your point of view, in forming permanent teams with the same members to structure one deal after another? Would that be better or worse than forming a new team for each new deal? Which would be better for the customer or client? Which would be better for you as an individual?

Managing Team Cohesion and Conflict at Baxter International

For nearly six years, Sue Ruley ruled over the warehouse occupied by Baxter International's Information Technology Group. She directed an organization of some 500 employees based in McGaw Park, Illinois, supporting Baxter's U.S. Healthcare Business. Ruley ordered 2,000-pound rolls of paper for printers that produce tens of thousands of Baxter invoices a week. She kept track of microfiche film, business forms, envelopes, computer components, and other supplies. And she decided when to order more. "I did everything, from top to bottom," she says.

Sue Ruley is known throughout Baxter's IT world today, not for her warehousing skills but as the team leader who helped to eliminate her own job. Ruley's team, one of about sixty IT teams the company formed in the 1990s, figured out how to eliminate warehouse duties by working with vendors to deliver supplies on a just-in-time basis. This decision, among others, saved the company more than $100,000 in the first year alone.

"In the past, management would decide what vendors to use and we had to smile and take it," Ruley says. "Sometimes that didn't go over real well. People didn't always feel we had the best product. By going to teams, we had control over who our vendors would be. We had more control over the product. And we came out way ahead moneywise." Hers sounds like a classic management-by-teams success story. And, in many respects, it has been. Ruley's team is typical of organizations that successfully move decision-making down to more appropriate levels. The demands on upper management are fewer, people closer to issues make the decisions that affect their own productivity, and the company saves money. How could anyone object?

"Going to teams," says Ruley, "meant a lot of difficult change, as well. Last year, for instance, we reduced staffing by about 10 percent." The result, she says, was increased suspicion and hurt feelings. "Not everybody was happy about the restructuring," according to Barbara Harmon, Baxter's IT Director of Human Resources. "We ended up being really very lean. We had a lot of talented individuals in the organization and we wanted a structure that would unleash that talent and get us closer to our customers." Baxter's newly structured IT work teams run the company's complex information network. And, aside from Ruley's support team, other IT teams write and troubleshoot computer programs, manage data, print reports, and send invoices.

"With teams, individual contributions from employees go up greatly," says Randy Johnson, one of Baxter's new IT team leaders. "It encourages employees to think and try new things—to take risks. Employees are given opportunities to grow and move in ways that they may not have had before." Teams have allowed Baxter IT to line up more closely with its customers, solving problems rapidly and generating ideas to help other business units work more efficiently. "You're empowered to do your job as best you can to meet Baxter's needs," Johnson says. "A business need will establish a deadline, but the rest is up to you."

So how does the company maximize a team's potential and deal with the conflict that is certain to arise in the new structure? Herb Walker, Senior Vice President for Human Resources, says Baxter is embracing teamwork throughout the company. While self-directed teams have played an important role in manufacturing for some time, only recently have they been introduced in sales, marketing, and staff functions like IT.

Walker hired two team-building specialists to address each of the issues the company knew would develop as teams were formed within and across functional lines. Tammy Van Valkenburgh, a team facilitator for IT, and Rob Reindl, a senior program manager from the Baxter Institute for Training and Development, went to work on the problem. "After a rocky beginning," says Reindl, "enthusiasm is rising. Employees are enjoying more autonomy, decision-making power, and influence over their own career development." Reindl added, "It's going to take three to five years to complete this change."

Reindl and colleague Van Valkenburgh developed a brief but important list of eight proactive methods for managing conflict in newly formed teams:

- **Speak Up:** Ask for what you need, whether it's information or equipment.
- **Share:** Distribute information you think others might need or want.
- **Trust:** Give people the benefit of the doubt regarding their intentions.

- **Make Friends:** Actively seek to build relationships on the team.
- **Plan:** Have an agenda, but be flexible.
- **Get Involved:** Participate and encourage others to do the same.
- **Respect Schedules:** Realize that everyone can't contribute to every project.
- **Be Candid:** Successful teams invite openness and honesty among members.

Team leader Sue Ruley adapted quickly, although not without a few bumps along the way. "When you're first learning the tools of working in teams, it seems like it takes forever," she recalls. "I was in so many team meetings, I was having a hard time getting my job done. But, in the long run," she added, "we saved time because we did things more efficiently." And, although she succeeded in phasing out her own job, Ruley feels fortunate. "They value enthusiasm and the ability to work in teams here," she says. "And Monday, I start training in a new area—telecommunication."

Source: M. Stott, "Going to Teams." *Pace,* an internal publication of Baxter Healthcare, Inc., September/October, 1994, 6–8.

QUESTIONS

1. Assuming you had been in Ms. Ruley's position when her supervisor approached her about transforming the structure of her workforce from a hierarchical staff to teams, what would you want to know before you agreed to the change? How would you deal with the uncertainty employees will feel following such changes?

2. How important do you think it is for members of a team to work in the same location? Should all of you be in the same office? On the same floor? In the same building?

3. How often would team members need to communicate with one another in order to respond to the needs of the company's clients in the U.S. Healthcare division?

4. How important would you regard face-to-face meetings with your own team members? What about meetings with customers? How frequently do you need to see them in person?

5. How comfortable would you feel in calling or speaking directly with a customer or member of your own organization who is substantially different from you in age and rank? What could you do to increase your comfort level—and that of the other person—in dealing with issues such as age, rank, status, and seniority?

6. What can teams do to increase the quality and rate of learning they experience? What would you suggest to Ms. Ruley as she forms a team to serve the needs of hospitals, clinics, and physicians' offices?

7. What's the value, from your point-of-view, in forming permanent teams with the same members to deal with the same customers on a long-term basis? Is there any value to organizing short-term teams just to deal with one-time issues or time-defined projects?

8. How would you advise Ms. Ruley to go about building trust among team members who have been accustomed to working in decidedly different organizational structures? How important is trust to the success of her team?

A TEAM COMMUNICATION RESOURCES

1. **Thomas-Kilmann Conflict Mode Instrument.** Xicom Incorporated, Sterling Forest, Tuxedo, NY 10987. Tel: 800-75-XICOM, or 914-351-4735.

2. **Myers-Briggs Type Indicator.** Consulting Psychologists Press, P.O. Box 10096, Palo Alto, CA 94303-0979. Tel: 800-624-1765.

3. **Discovery Learning Products.** P.O. Box 20304, Greensboro, NC 27420. Tel: 910-272-9530.

4. **Campbell-Hallam Team Development Survey.** *http://www.ncs.com.* Tel: 847-292-1900.

5. **Group Styles Inventory.** Human Synergistics, *http://www.hsnz.co.nz.* Tel: 847-590-0995.

6. **Personal Profile System®** from the Carlson Learning Company. Local distributors available by calling 1-800-777-9897.

7. **Team Climate Inventory.** Hanover House, UK. Tel: 44 1753 850333.

SELECT BIBLIOGRAPHY

Adler, Nancy. *International Dimensions of Organizational Behavior*. Cincinnati: South-Western College Publishing, 1997.

Amason, A. C., and H. J. Sapienza. "The Effects of Top Management Team Size and Interaction Norms on Cognitive and Affective Conflict." *Journal of Management* 23, no. 4 (1997): 495–516.

Argyris, Chris. "Teaching Smart People How to Learn." *Harvard Business Review* (May–June 1991).

Barsky, Allan Edward. *Conflict Resolution for the Helping Professions*. Belmont, CA: Brooks/Cole, 2000.

Bernstein, A., P. Galuszka, and R. Barker. "What Price Peace? GM Lost a Lot to the UAW, and Labor Relations Are Still Bad." *BusinessWeek,* August 10, 1998, 24–25.

Bettenhausen, K. L. "Five Years of Groups Research: What We Have Learned and What Needs to be Addressed." *Journal of Management* 17, no. 2 (1991): 345–381.

Boulding, K. *Conflict and Defense*. New York: Harper & Row, 1963.

Byrne, John A. "Visionary vs. Visionary." *BusinessWeek,* August 28, 2000, 212.

Capozzoli, Thomas K. "Conflict Resolution: A Key Ingredient in Successful Teams." *Supervision* 11 (Nov. 1999): 60.

Cohen, Susan G., and Diane E. Bailey. "What Makes Teams Work: Group Effectiveness Research from the Shop Floor to the Executive Suite." *Journal of Management* 23, no. 3 (1997): 239–290.

Cox, Jr., Taylor. *Cultural Diversity in Organizations: Theory, Research, and Practice*. San Francisco: Berrett-Koehler, 1993.

Cusumano, Michael A. "How Microsoft Makes Large Teams Work Like Small Teams." *Sloan Management Review* (fall 1997).

Daly, Kristin, and Herminia Ibarra. "Gender Differences in Managerial Behavior: The Ongoing Debate." Harvard Business School 9-494-038, March 12, 1995.

Deming, W. Edwards. *The New Economics for Industry, Government, Education*. Cambridge, MA: MIT Center for Advanced Engineering Study, 1993.

Donnellon, Anne. *Team Talk: The Power of Language in Team Dynamics*. Boston: Harvard Business School Press, 2000.

Druskat, Vaness Urch, and Steven B. Wolff. "Building the Emotional Intelligence of Groups." *Harvard Business Review* (March 2001): 81–90.

D'Souza, Dinesh. "Lottery of Success." *Business 2.0,* December 12, 2000, 218–235.

Gefen, David, and Detmar W. Straub, "Gender Differences in the Perception and Use of E-mail: An Extension to the Technology Acceptance Model." *MIS Quarterly* 21, no. 1 (1997): 389–400.

Gentile, Mary C., ed. *Managerial Excellence Through Diversity.* Prospect Heights, IL: Waveland Press, 1996.

Gigone, D., and R. Hastie. "The Common Knowledge Effect: Information Sharing and Group Judgment." *Journal of Personality and Social Psychology* 72, no. 1 (1993): 132–140.

Girard, Kim. "Return of the Crummy Job." *Business 2.0,* February 6, 2001, 75.

Goodman, Paul S. *Designing Effective Work Groups.* San Francisco: Jossey-Bass, 1986.

Gross, Michael A., and Laura K. Guerrero. "Managing Conflict Appropriately and Effectively: An Application of the Competence Model to Rahim's Organizational Conflict Styles." *International Journal of Conflict Management* 11, no. 3 (2000): 200–226.

Hackman, R. J., ed. *Groups That Work (and Those That Don't): Creating Conditions for Effective Teamwork.* San Francisco: Jossey-Bass, 1990.

Hackman, R. J., and R. E. Walton, "Leading Groups in Organizations." In *Designing Effective Work Groups,* edited by P. S. Goodman. San Francisco: Jossey-Bass, 1986, 72–119.

Hambrick, David, S. C. Davison, S. A. Snell, and C. C. Snow. *When Groups Consist of Multiple Nationalities: Toward a New Understanding of the Implications.* Report available from the International Consortium for Executive Development, Lexington, MA.

Hambrick, Donald C., David A. Nadler, Michael L. Tushman, eds. *Negotiating Change: How CEOs, Top Teams, and Boards Steer Transformation.* Boston: Harvard Business School Press, 1998.

Harvey, J. "The Abilene Paradox: The Management of Agreement." *Organizational Dynamics* 1, no. 3 (1974): 63–80.

Hill, L. A. *Building Effective One-on-One Work Relationships.* Harvard Business School reprint, 9-497-028, October 13, 1996.

Hill, L. A. *Managing Your Team.* Harvard Business School Teaching Note 9-494-081, rev. March 28, 1995.

Hirschhorn, L. *Managing in the New Team Environment: Skills, Tools, and Methods.* Reading, MA: Addison-Wesley, 1991.

Jehn, Karen A. "Enhancing Effectiveness: An Investigation of Advantages and Disadvantages of Value-Based Intragroup Conflict." *International Journal of Conflict Management* 5, no. 3 (July 1994): 223–238.

Jehn, Karen, and Elizabeth A. Mannix. "The Dynamic Nature of Conflict: A Longitudinal Study of Intragroup Conflict and Group Performance." *Academy of Management Journal* 44, no. 2 (April 2001): 238–252.

Kanter, Rosabeth M. *Men and Women of the Corporation,* 2nd ed. New York: Basic Books, 1993.

Katzenbach, J. R. *Teams at the Top: Unleashing the Potential of Both Teams and Individual Leaders.* Boston: Harvard Business School Press, 1998.

Katzenbach, J. R., and D. K. Smith. "The Discipline of Teams." *Harvard Business Review* (March–April, 1993), 111–124.

Katzenbach, J. R., and D. K. Smith. *The Wisdom of Teams: Creating the High-Performance Organization.* New York: HarperCollins, 1993, rpt. 1999.

Kling, J. "Tension in Teams: When Is It Destructive, When Is It Creative?" *Harvard Management Communication Letter* 3, no. 7 (July 2000): 1–3.

Kotter, John. *What Leaders Really Do.* Boston: Harvard Business School Press, 1999.

Larson, C. E., and Frank M. J. LaFasto. *Team Work: What Must Go Right/What Can Go Wrong.* Newbury Park, CA: Sage, 1989, 84.

Lawler, E. E., III, S. A. Mohrman, and G. E. Ledford, Jr. *Creating High Performance Organizations: Practices and Results of Employee Involvement and Total Quality Management in Fortune 1000 Companies.* San Francisco: Jossey-Bass, 1995.

Mandel, Michael J., and Robert D. Hof. "Rethinking the Internet." *BusinessWeek,* March 26, 2001.

Maruca, Regina. "What Makes Teams Work?" *Fast Company* 35 (November 2000).

Maznevski, M. L. "Understanding Our Differences: Performance in Decision-Making Groups with Diverse Members." *Human Relations* 47, no. 5 (1994): 531–552.

Mohrman, S. A., S. G. Cohen, and A. M. Morhman. *Designing Team-Based Organizations: New Forms for Knowledge Work.* San Francisco: Jossey-Bass, 1995.

Moran, Susan. "Minimum Tax, Maximum Headache." *Business 2.0,* February 6, 2001, 79.

Mulvey, P. W., J. F. Viega, and P. M. Elsass. "When Teammates Raise a White Flag." *Academy of Management Executive* 10, no. 1 (1996): 40–49.

Nadler, D. A., J. L. Spencer, and Associates, eds. *Executive Teams.* San Francisco: Jossey-Bass, 1997.

Nadler, J., L. Thompson, and M. Morris. "Schmooze or Lose: The Efforts of Rapport and Gender in E-mail Negotiations." Paper Presented at the Academy of Management Annual Conference, August 1999, Chicago, IL.

Nelson, Mariah Burton. "Learning What 'Team' Really Means." *Newsweek,* July 19, 1999, 55.

Nicotera, A. M., ed. *Conflict and Organizations: Communicative Processes.* Albany, NY: State University of New York Press, 1995.

Orbe, M. P., and T. M. Harris. *Interracial Communication: Theory Into Practice.* Belmont, CA: Wadsworth/Thomson Learning, 2001, 7.

O'Rourke, James S., IV. *Management Communication: A Case Analysis Approach.* Upper Saddle River, NJ: Prentice-Hall, 2000.

Papa, M. J., and D. J. Canary. "Conflict in Organizations: A Competence-Based Approach." In *Conflict and Organizations: Communicative Processes,* edited by A. M. Nicotera. Albany, NY: State University of New York Press, 1995.

Pelled, L. H. "Demographic Diversity, Conflict, and Work Group Outcomes: An Intervening Process Theory." *Organization Science* 7, no. 6 (1996): 615–631.

Rahim, M. A., and T. V. Bonoma. "Managing Organizational Conflict: A Model for Diagnosis and Intervention." *Psychological Reports* 44 (1979): 36–48.

Robbins, S. P. *Organizational Behavior: Concepts, Controversies, and Applications,* 8th ed. Upper Saddle River, NJ: Prentice-Hall, 1998.

Seglin, Jeffrey L. "When to Go Along, and When to Walk Away." *The New York Times,* Sunday, February 18, 2001, 4BU.

Senge, Peter M. *The Fifth Discipline.* New York: Doubleday Currency, 1990.

Smith, K. G., K. A. Smith, J. D. Olian, H. P. Smis, Jr., D. P. O'Bannon, and J. A. Scully. "Top Management Team Demography and Process: The Role of Social Integration and Communication." *Administration Science Quarterly* 39 (1994): 412–438.

Steinhauer, Jennifer. "So, the Tumor Is On the Left, Right? Seeking Ways to Reduce Operating Room Errors." *The New York Times,* April 1, 2001, A-23.

Stott, M. "Going to Teams." *Pace,* an internal publication of Baxter Healthcare, Inc., September/October, 1994, 6–8.

Suchan, J., and R. Colucci. "An Analysis of Communication Efficiency between High-Impact and a Bureaucratic Written Communication." *Management Communication Quarterly* 2 (May 1989): 454–484.

Tannen, Deborah. "The Power of Talk: Who Gets Heard and Why." *Harvard Business Review,* September–October 1995, 138–148.

Tannenbaum, R., and W. H. Schmidt. "How to Choose a Leadership Pattern." *Harvard Business Review* (May–June 1973): 162–170.

Thomas, David A., and Robin J. Ely. "Making Differences Matter: A New Paradigm for Managing Diversity." *Harvard Business Review* (September–October 1996): 79–90.

Thomas, K. W. "Conflict and Negotiation Processes in Organizations." In vol. 3 of *Handbook of Industrial and Organizational Psychology,* 2nd ed., edited by M. D. Dunnette and L. M. Hough. Palo Alto, CA: Consulting Psychologists Press, 1994.

Thompson, L. *Making the Team: A Guide for Managers.* Upper Saddle River, NJ: Prentice-Hall, 2000, 217–218.

Tuckman, Bruce W. "Development Sequence in Small Groups." *Psychological Bulletin* 63, no. 6 (1965): 384–399.

Watson, W. E., K. Kumar, and L. K. Michaelsen. "Cultural Diversity's Impact on Interaction Process and Performance: Comparing Homogeneous and Diverse Task Groups." *Academy of Management Journal* 36 (1993): 590–602.

Wegner, D. M. "Transactive Memory: A Contemporary Analysis of the Group Mind." In *Theories of Group Behavior,* edited by B. Mullen and G. Goethals. New York: Springer-Verlag, 1986, 185–208.

Whetten, D. A., and K. S. Cameron. *Developing Management Skills: Managing Conflict.* New York: HarperCollins, 1993.